IP Subnetting
From Zero to Guru

Paul Browning

TECHNICAL EDITORS

Thanks to the below technical editors who donated their time to improve this book.

John DeGennaro	Mario Salinas	Charles Burkholder
Steve Quan	Elmarine Jimenez	Thierry Merle
Frank Faith	Charles Pacheco	Jeff Echano
John S. Galliano	Timothy A. Clark	Carol Wood
Michael A. Sisson	Roy Thelin	Ellsworth Wilson
Georgia E. Jaeger	Tim Peel	

ALSO FROM REALITY PRESS

101 Labs – Cisco CCNA
101 Labs – CompTIA Network+
101 Labs – IP Subnetting
Cisco CCNA Simplified
Cisco CCNA in 60 Days

Table of Contents

Subnetting—What Is It and Why Learn It?

Good question. Let me ask you one back. Are you in the IT industry already, or are you hoping to get into the IT industry and in particular into some sort of helpdesk, PC support, networking, or other technical role?

Subnetting is used all over the world on almost every network (including your home network). It's the process of taking a standard network address and making smaller (sub)networks from it. It's just like cutting a cake into slices, but we are doing it with address ranges instead of food.

Unfortunately, there are special rules you need to follow in order to avoid getting into trouble and assigning the incorrect address to the wrong device or part of your network. These rules have been frustrating IT students and engineers for decades.

When I started consulting in IT, I found to my horror that around 95% of IT people didn't actually know how IP addressing and subnetting actually work. They relied on online calculators to answer any problems. These won't help you in exams, job interviews, or if your boss or customer is standing over you as you try to fix an IP addressing issue.

If you want to be in the IT industry, you must understand how to subnet. You will be challenged on subnetting questions in:

- Job interviews for IT roles
- Carrying out your IT job
- Any IT exam you want to pass

In fact, subnetting questions will form around 9% of your final score in most IT exams.

I spent many weeks trying to learn the process of subnetting when I started studying for the CCNA exam. I took the exam and failed miserably, my (lack of) understanding of IP subnetting letting me down.

A few years later I began teaching IT courses and invented my own way of subnetting. This easy way to subnet will get you through any IT exam, technical interview, or real-world subnetting problem. If you spend just a few hours reading this book and following my examples, you will be able to subnet very quickly and accurately. I guarantee it in fact.

Your Subnetting Journey

Just the same as learning how to drive or ride a bike, you need learn how to subnet only once. After that I recommend spending around one hour per month brushing up on my easy subnetting method so you stay sharp.

What you'll learn in the next few hours will help you for years to come. I know that very well as understanding how to subnet has been a huge help to me from working on a helpdesk, doing network support, and eventually consulting for large companies. When I started teaching networking and Cisco courses, I shared this method with others, who found it equally useful.

In this book you will learn how network addressing works and how to easily and quickly determine which subnet a particular host belongs to. You will learn how to quickly and easily resolve IP addressing issues while other engineers around you are busy surfing the net looking for subnet calculators.

Together we will run through the basic building blocks of subnetting, including binary math, powers of two, and IP address classes. We will then go through the long way of working out subnets so you can see how it all works. We will then move on to the superfast way to answer questions in IT exams and technical interviews. This method will get you the answer to most subnetting questions in under 60 seconds.

You will avoid the embarrassment of having to troubleshoot IP addressing issues on a live network but not knowing where to start. I've been in situations where colleagues were left red-faced at work because they couldn't subnet.

For my job interview for Cisco Systems I was asked by two senior network engineers to answer subnetting questions on a whiteboard. The questions lasted for about 45 minutes. I used the easy method you will learn here to answer all the questions.

You will discover how to avoid common mistakes that have cost many network engineers their jobs (I've seen it happen), and mistakes many exam candidates make when answering subnetting questions.

You are going to learn what most network engineers skip, overlook, or simply don't know. By the end of this journey you will know more than 95% of network engineers currently employed in the IT industry! I should know—I have worked on hundreds of networks and met over a thousand IT engineers throughout my time as a Cisco TAC specialist and through my Cisco and networking training courses.

You'll be very surprised at just how easy all this stuff really is. It really isn't complicated at all to be honest (once you see the easy way to subnet). The problem for many years has been that very technical people have tried to make something that is easy appear very difficult. Why they do that I will never know. Perhaps they want other people to think that subnetting is some mysterious skill that only a few engineers can master, or perhaps they understand something only when it is explained in a complicated way.

Does all this sound too good to be true? Let me take what is seemingly a huge and complicated subject and show you how easy it all really is.

Introduction to 2018 Edition

It's hard to believe that I first wrote this book in 2006. So much has changed since then, including my having three children and emigrating from the UK to Australia.

So much has also changed in the world of IT. Cloud computing has exploded onto the scene, and IPv6 is now ubiquitous. As an IT engineer you are expected to know so much more now. Whereas back in the day you could afford to be an expert in just one area, now the typical IT person should know about wireless, IPv6, security, cloud, mobile technology, IoT, and much more.

Thankfully, certifications such as CompTIA Network+ cover all of this and more.

IP subnetting is extensively tested now, more than ever. In every IT exam from Cisco, CompTIA, Microsoft, Amazon, Juniper, Wireshark, and others, you must have a strong grasp of subnetting principles. You are also now tested on IPv6 concepts, which proves an entirely new challenge.

This new edition reflects changes from feedback I've had from the many thousands of students who have used my easy subnetting method to pass their exams, ace technical job interviews, and solve problems at work as an IT engineer.

About Me

I served as a police officer in the UK for 12 years. I was in uniform on the streets as a police constable and then served as a detective. I was promoted after about 7 years to sergeant and worked in uniform in Birmingham for 5 years before leaving for a career in IT. I worked on a helpdesk for a while and studied hard, and over a period of several years I passed my MCSE, A+, Network+, CCNA, and CCNP and then my CCIE written exams. Just for the record, I find studying really hard, so for every hour everybody else was putting in I had to do two.

I eventually got a job at the Cisco TAC, where I worked for 2 years doing router architecture support and then WAN support. We were all made redundant in 2002, so I started my own IT consultancy and training company. I now own www.howtonetwork.com, which teaches IT certification courses via video, and www.101labs.net, which is a hands-on IT training site that is all practical and zero theory.

I am not a naturally technical person and I find it difficult to absorb information, so what I tend to do is try to make it all as easy as possible to understand. I always found subnetting to be particularly challenging; you may find it hard too.

I read several subnetting books written by people touted as IT 'experts', but I was left more confused than when I started. I read several CCNA books, paid for CD-ROMs from websites, and read white papers, but they made it all sound so complicated. I thought to myself there must be an easier way than this to learn how to subnet. I was right, but I didn't realize that I would be the one to discover it!

After weeks of frustration I penciled out a few subnetting ideas myself and quite by accident discovered a very simple, accurate, and easy way to work out subnetting problems. I also developed the Subnetting Cheat Chart, which you will see explained in great detail in Part 2. This is the exact method I've used for years to teach the students in my classroom courses and IT books.

How the Books Are Laid Out

You start with the basics, such as binary math, hexadecimal, and how to convert between that and decimal. You learn where subnetting actually comes from and why. You will learn the longhand way of working out subnetting problems before progressing (in Part 2) to learn the quick and easy way which I recommend you use in exams, IT interviews, and troubleshooting live network issues, where time is of the essence.

WHAT YOU WILL LEARN IN PART 1

- How binary works—Why do we have to bring in binary math to confuse everything? Well, you will learn why we use it, how to quickly determine binary addresses, and how to convert them to decimal.

- How hexadecimal works—If you want to pass the CCNA or Network+ exam, you will need to understand hex numbering. I explain how it all works and more.

- IP addressing—What is an IP address made from, what is an octet, why are IP addresses broken down into classes, and why are classes not important anymore?

- How to subnet—The reason why you bought the book in the first place! You will be guided step by step through how to determine which subnet a certain host is in. This is the longer way, which you need to understand before moving on to the quick and easy way in Part 2.

- How to supernet a network when advertising it to the internet

WHAT YOU WILL LEARN IN PART 2

- 20 examples of Class A, B, and C subnets with as many different subnet masks as I could think of. By the time you have worked through every example several times, you will be supremely confident in subnetting.

- Subnetting in your head—No, I am not mad! You will see that it is actually possible to work out subnetting problems in your head without putting pen to paper. Wait and see.

- Network design—If you were asked by a client or your boss to create a subnet mask which generates 6 subnets with at least 20 hosts per subnet, could you come up with the answer in about 10 seconds? You will learn how here.

- IPv6 addressing and subnetting

- Using wildcard masks

By the end of Part 2 you will have a firm grasp of all subnetting principles and be able to apply everything you know in exams and real-world situations.

SUBNETTING VIDEO COURSE

For those of you who want to take the video course please check out the below URL. You certainly don't need to take it, but if you do, please do put the code 'subnetting' into the coupon box to get access for 30 days for just $1.

The website also features over 25 IT certification and career courses.

https://www.howtonetwork.com/courses/tcp-ip/
ip-subnetting-zero-to-guru/

How to Read These Books

Did you know that the way we are taught to learn in school is probably the worst method possible! Have you ever just sat there staring at a book trying to force the information in or reading a few pages and completely forgetting what you have just read? Our recall is less than 40% an hour later and less than 20% 24 hours later.

May I be so humble to suggest that trying to force new information into your brain by staring at the page and hoping it sinks in won't work? Try the following way instead and see how much your understanding and retention improves.

Step 1—Flick through every page in Part 1 and Part 2, just glancing over it and not actually reading the text. Just pick up the main headers and subjects covered. Take no more than about 5 seconds per page.

Step 2—Flick through the pages again, but this time spending about 10 seconds per page and glancing at the first few sentences under each main heading.

Step 3—Do the same again, but this time take about 30 seconds. Casually take in the main themes of each page and a few sentences as well. Enjoy the process and tell yourself that you don't really care how much information goes in or how quickly.

Step 4—Take a break and do something else. Subnetting is a skill you will have for life, so there is no hurry.

Step 5—This time have a more thorough read through each page. Take about 1 minute per page and avoid subvocalizing (reading the words out in your head as if you were speaking out loud). Reading out the words in your head is actually going to slow you down quite a bit.

Make a mental note of the content and subject matter, but let it soak in at the speed that feels natural for you. The mind has 100% perfect retention and picks up every sentence, word, and letter. The bit we sometimes struggle with is the recall!

Step 6—Take about 2 minutes per page, and if it helps, put a small tick next to the areas of major interest to you. Enjoy the process.

Take a break and the next day do Step 6 again. Keep following Step 6 and as you pass over the pages time and time again, you will find that the material goes in effortlessly. You will also find that you have the ability to recall and apply the information with amazing accuracy.

Set a goal to spend about 20 minutes per day (no more than 30) learning the material. You wouldn't expect to learn juggling in an hour, so why expect to understand all of this in the same time? Let the knowledge sink in at the right pace for you to be sure it stays in. I know that this is the easy way to subnet, but it isn't a quick fix. You must still invest some time to learn how to apply the skills.

If you want to learn more about speed reading, I recommend Evelyn Woods's speed reading books or home study course if you can find it on the web or on eBay. It will be time well invested.

Part 1

IP Addressing

HOW BINARY WORKS

In order to understand how IP addressing works you need to understand binary mathematics (unfortunately). Computers and networking equipment do not understand decimal. We use decimal because it is a numbering system that uses 10 digits. It was invented by a caveman centuries ago when he realized we all have 10 digits on our hands and they could be used for counting buffalo as they walked past his cave.

Computers and networking equipment can only understand electrical signals. Since an electrical signal can only be on or off, the only numbering system that will work is binary. Binary uses only two numbers, 0 or 1. A 0 means there is no electrical pulse on the wire, and a 1 means that there is.

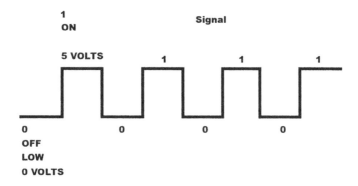

Fig. 1.1—Volts on or Off

The pulse in the above figure would be received as electrical signals by a PC (for example) and converted to 01010101 and then to a decimal value (85) so we could read it and understand it.

Any number can be made up from binary values. The more binary values we add, the larger the number. If we want to convert binary to decimal, we need some sort of counting method to match binary to decimal.

In order to do this, we start at number 1 and then for every binary value we add we double the decimal value—i.e., 1 to 2 to 4 to 8 to 16 and so on into infinity if we wish, but we start on the right and move left. It's easiest to do this by writing two rows with the decimal at the top and binary underneath.

You can see below that with two binary digits we can count up to 3 in decimal. We just place a 0 or a 1 in the column to decide if we want to use that value or not.

We will start with only two binary values in the columns, 1 and 2 to the left. The top row is the decimal, with the binary values underneath, which can be turned on or off by adding a 1 or 0.

2	1
0	0

$$0 + 0 = 0$$

2	1
0	1

$$0 + 1 = 1$$

2	1
1	0

$$2 + 0 = 2$$

2	1
1	1

$$2 + 1 = 3$$

If we use 8 binary bit places (an octet), we can get any number from 0 up to 255. You can see that we start our numbering from the right and move across to the left.

128	64	32	16	8	4	2	1

If we add a 0 to each of these columns, we have a value of 0 in decimal.

128	64	32	16	8	4	2	1
0	0	0	0	0	0	0	0

If we add a 1 to each of these columns, we have a value of 255 in decimal.

128	64	32	16	8	4	2	1
1	1	1	1	1	1	1	1

Don't believe me?

$$128 + 64 + 32 + 16 + 8 + 4 + 2 + 1 = 255$$

So logic dictates we can actually make any number from 0 to 255 by placing an on or off bit (a 0 or a 1) in the various columns.

128	64	32	16	8	4	2	1
0	0	1	0	1	1	0	0

$$32 + 8 + 4 = 44$$

The octet is ubiquitous in IT, and as you've seen, it's made from 8 bits. Four octets are used for an IPv4 address, which, as you will see, turned out to be insufficient for modern requirements. Half an octet is 4 bits and is referred to as a nibble, although it's pretty rare to hear this term nowadays.

IP addressing and subnetting are based on the fundamentals above. We can summarize what we know so far by looking at Table 1.1. Pay special attention to this because the values can be used for any subnet mask (more on this later).

In this table I start on the left and add 1 in each line. This is where the subnet numbers come from in your octets.

Binary	Decimal
10000000	128
11000000	192
11100000	224
11110000	240
11111000	248
11111100	252
11111110	254
11111111	255

Table 1.1—Binary values

Make up some of your own binary numbers to ensure you understand this fully. Feel free to search for some binary teaching apps, such as Binary Grid Puzzle – Math Game.

In exams such as CompTIA Network+, A+, and CCNA you can expect to be asked to convert binary to decimal or decimal to hex.

HOW HEXADECIMAL WORKS

Hexadecimal (or hex) is an alternative numbering system. Rather than counting in twos or tens, 16 numbers or characters are used. Hex starts at 0 and goes all the way up to F:

0 1 2 3 4 5 6 7 8 9 A B C D E F

Each hexadecimal digit actually represents four binary digits.

Decimal	0	1	2	3	4	5	6	7
Hex	0	1	2	3	4	5	6	7
Binary	0000	0001	0010	0011	0100	0101	0110	0111
Decimal	8	9	10	11	12	13	14	15
Hex	8	9	A	B	C	D	E	F
Binary	1000	1001	1010	1011	1100	1101	1110	1111

Table 1.2—Binary to hex to decimal conversion

Converting binary to hex is fairly simple.

Decimal	13	6	2	12
Hex	D	6	2	C
Binary	1101	0110	0010	1100

Hex is a counting system more manageable for humans than binary but close enough to binary to be used by computers and networking equipment. Any number can be made using hex, as with binary and decimal. We just count in multiples of 16 instead: 1, then 16, then 16 multiplied by 16 (256), then 256 multiplied by 16 (4096), and so on.

	4096	256	16	1
Hex			1	A

Counting in hex therefore goes 0 1 2 3 4 5 6 7 8 9 A B C D E F 10 11 12 13 14 15 16 17 18 19 1A 1B 1C 1D 1E 1F 20 21 22 etc. to infinity. 1A (above), for example, is an A in the 1 column and a 1 in the 16 column: A = 10 + 16 = 26.

When converting binary to hex, it makes the task easier to break the octet into two groups of 4 bits. So 11110011 becomes 1111 0011. 1111 is 8 + 4 + 2 + 1 = 15 and 0011 is 2 + 1 = 3. 15 is F in hex and 3 is 3 in hex, giving us the answer F3. You can check Table 1.2 (above) to confirm this.

Hex to binary is the same process. 7C can be split into 7, which is 0111 in binary, and C, which is (12 in decimal or) 1100 in binary. The answer is 01111100.

Hex is used exclusively in IPv6 addressing because the size of the address is 128 bits, which would be next to impossible to write out in binary. Here is an example from Wikipedia:

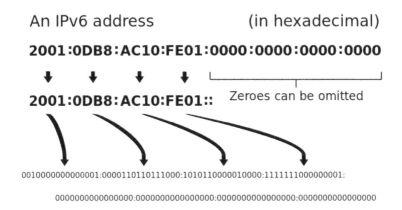

Fig. 1.2—An IPv6 address in hex and binary. Reprinted from Wikipedia

We will refer to hexadecimal once again when we cover IPv6 addressing.

HAVE A TRY

Here are some examples for you to try. If you get stuck, you can find the answers overleaf. A very useful thing to do would be to write out the charts for working out hex and binary—i.e., for hex a 1 column, then a 16 column, then a 256 column, and so on.

1. Convert 1111 from binary to hex and decimal.
2. Convert 11010 from binary to hex and decimal.
3. Convert 10000 from binary to hex and decimal.
4. Convert 20 from decimal to binary and hex.
5. Convert 32 from decimal to binary and hex.
6. Convert 101 from decimal to binary and hex.
7. Convert A6 from hex to binary and decimal.
8. Convert 15 from hex to binary and decimal.
9. Convert B5 from hex to binary and decimal.

It would be useful in any IT exam to write out Table 1.2 to help you work out any binary to hex to decimal conversions.

Conversion Answers

Convert 1111 from binary to hex and decimal:
Hex = F; Decimal = 15

Convert 11010 from binary to hex and decimal:
Hex = 1A; Decimal = 26

Convert 10000 from binary to hex and decimal:
Hex = 10; Decimal = 16

Convert 20 from decimal to binary and hex:
Binary = 10100; Hex = 14

Convert 32 from decimal to binary and hex:
Binary = 100000; Hex = 20

Convert 101 from decimal to binary and hex:
Binary = 1100101; Hex = 65

Convert A6 from hex to binary and decimal:
Binary = 10100110; Decimal = 166

Convert 15 from hex to binary and decimal:
Binary = 10101; Decimal = 21

Convert B5 from hex to binary and decimal:
Binary = 10110101; Decimal = 181

IP Version 4

The current version of the Internet Protocol (IP) in wide deployment is version 4. Version 6 is currently in use on around 50% of all networks and will ultimately replace IPv4 on the internet. It is important to understand that although most IT exams are concerned with subnetting in IPv4, you should be familiar with how to read IPv6 (see later section) because at some point in the not too distant future it will become the standard for all networks.

IPv4 uses four octets in a group to create an IP address and each octet is made up of 8 bits or 1 byte. Therefore every IP address is 32 binary bits (4 × 8 = 32) or 4 bytes.

> **FOR EXAMS**: You may see questions that ask about IP addressing in either bits or bytes; pay careful attention and read the question thoroughly.

IPv4 was designed so that there would be enough IP addresses for the foreseeable future. No one predicted the huge growth in IT that was to come, so this scheme in its initial incarnation had to be amended to cater for the demand.

An example of how an IPv4 address appears in binary:

11000011.11110000.11001011.11111100
1st octet   2nd octet   3rd octet   4th octet

Each grouping of eight numbers is an octet, and the four octets give us a 32-bit IP address.

IN THE REAL WORLD: It is worth remembering that routers and PCs do not see an IPv4 address as four octets; they just see 32 bits. Octets just make things easier for us to see.

POWERS OF TWO

In order to really understand IP addressing you should understand the powers of two. While it may appear confusing initially, you simply start with the number 2 and keep doubling the previous number. That's all there is to it.

$1 \times 2 = 2$
$2 \times 2 = 4$
$4 \times 2 = 8$
$8 \times 2 = 16$

The important thing isn't the multiplication; it is what is happening to the answers. Each time, the number doubles. If we want to work out the powers, we would write them like this:

$2^1 = 2 \times 1$, which is 2
$2^2 = 2 \times 2$, which is 4
$2^3 = 2 \times 2 \times 2$, which is 8
$2^4 = 2 \times 2 \times 2 \times 2$, which is 16
$2^5 = 2 \times 2 \times 2 \times 2 \times 2$, which is 32
and so on.

This process will become important when you are asked to work out how many subnets and hosts per subnet are generated with a particular subnet mask.

IP ADDRESSING

So now we understand that an IP address is made up from binary numbers which are grouped into octets. The reason for this is that when IP addressing was first conceived, it was determined that this number would be more than enough for many years to come. Unfortunately, the huge growth of home and mobile devices and business computing was never anticipated. IPv6 has 340 trillion trillion trillion available addresses, so that should last well into the future.

IP (version 4) addresses are broken down into classes. Classes were used when IP addresses were first developed. How large your organization was, dictated which class of IP address you were given. Large organizations were allocated Class A, medium ones Class B, and small ones Class C.

> **IN THE REAL WORLD**: IP addresses are assigned by a group called the IANA (Internet Assigned Numbers Authority). You can also buy one from an ISP that has bought a block from the IANA.

Class A Addresses

Historically, these were given to the largest organizations, which would need a tremendous number of IP addresses since they owned more computers than everyone else. Class A addresses use only the first octet to identify the network number. The remaining three octets are left for identifying the hosts on the network.

Network.Host.Host.Host
10.2.5.4

So the network is 10 and 2.5.4 is a host on that network.

In binary it would look like:

nnnnnnnn.hhhhhhhh.hhhhhhhh.hhhhhhhh
00001010.00000010.00000101.00000100

IN THE REAL WORLD: You would pronounce the above IP address as 'ten dot two dot five dot four'.

Class A addresses are numbered 1 to 126 in the first octet. Network equipment identifies a Class A address because the very first bit in the first octet has to be a 0. A Class A address cannot have a 1 in this bit position.

So the first network number is 1.

128	64	32	16	8	4	2	1
0	0	0	0	0	0	0	1

The last possible network number is 127 (check by adding all the values together). Network number 127 cannot actually be used because the value 127.0.0.1 is reserved for troubleshooting. You can ping the loopback address to check if TCP/IP is working on your host.

128	64	32	16	8	4	2	1
0	1	1	1	1	1	1	1

We are not permitted to use 0 as a network number or 127, which leaves us 126 available networks for Class A addresses. You may already recognize the 127 network address because if you ping IP address 127.0.0.1, you are actually pinging your own machine to test whether TCP/IP is correctly installed.

For the hosts we can start at number 1 until every single possible value is used up. We will use an address starting with 10 to illustrate the example.

10.0.0.1 is the first host, or in binary:

00001010.00000000.00000000.00000001
10.   0.   0.   1

10.0.0.2 is the second host, or in binary:

00001010.00000000.00000000.00000010
10.   0.   0.   2.

10.255.255.254 is the last host, or in binary:

00001010.11111111.11111111.11111110

Now you can see why we use decimal. It would take a long time to write out addresses in binary, and be almost impossible to remember them. You can change Cisco router settings to display all addresses in binary, but there is no reason ever to do this.

Why can't we have 10.255.255.255 as a host? Because when all the binary values have a 1 in the host part of the address, this tells the network that it is a broadcast packet. We will learn how this works later.

Class B Addresses

Class B addresses were reserved for large organizations that needed a lot of host numbers but not as many as the largest ones. Unfortunately, when a Class B address was assigned to an organization, it resulted in thousands of wasted host addresses.

Class B addresses have to have the first two binary values in the first octet reserved with a 1 and a 0 next to it.

So the first network number is 128. We have all the available network bits in the first octet turned off.

128	64	32	16	8	4	2	1
1	0	0	0	0	0	0	0

The last available Class B network number is 191 (add the values together). Here we have turned the all network bits on (in the first octet).

128	64	32	16	8	4	2	1
1	0	1	1	1	1	1	1

For Class B addresses we use the first two octets for the network address. For example, in the address 130.24.5.2, 130.24 is the network number and

5.2 is a host on that network. The rule still is that the first number you see will always be between 128 and 191 inclusive.

If we use the powers of two rule, in the first two octets we will see that we can have a possible 65,536 (2^{16}) networks. We are, however, not allowed to use the first 2 bits of the first octet because they are reserved for showing the 10 (binary) value, remember? So this leaves us with 6 + 8 digits. 2^{14} gives us 16,384 networks.

We have the full two octets to use for hosts, so 8 + 8 bits gives us $2^{16} =$ 65,536 hosts per Class B network. We actually have to take 2 away from this value for the broadcast and subnet (more on this later), so technically it is 65,534 host addresses.

This will start to make more sense as we work through some subnetting and network design examples. We're just laying the foundation at the moment.

Class C Addresses

These were originally reserved for any organization that was not large enough to warrant having a Class A or B address. A Class C address has the first 3 bits reserved, so the network device can recognize it as such. The first 3 bits must show as 110.

The first network number is 192. All the other network bits are off (0).

128	64	32	16	8	4	2	1
1	1	0	0	0	0	0	0

The last is 223. This time all the network bits are on (in the first octet).

128	64	32	16	8	4	2	1
1	1	0	1	1	1	1	1

An example of a Class C address is 200.2.1.4: 200.2.1 is the network address and .4 is a host on that network. So we can see that there are lots of available network numbers to assign to companies; however, we have a limited quantity of numbers that are free to use for the hosts on our networks.

For Class C networks we have to take the first 3 bits (110) from the first octet, giving us $5 + 8 + 8 = 21$ (network bits).

$2^{21} = 2,097,152$

For the hosts we have 2^8, giving us 256 per network (only 254 are usable though).

INSPIRATION: If none of this makes any sense at the moment, this is only to be expected. I read the subnetting chapter in a very popular CCNA book for six weeks and it still made no sense to me. Eventually I worked out the easy way to subnet, which I will share with you later. It is simply a case of reading through this material several (or more) times for it to start to make more and more sense.

Class D and Class E Addresses

Class D addresses are reserved for multicast traffic and cannot be used on your network. Multicast traffic is traffic sent to multiple hosts using one IP address. A live webcast of a rock concert is an example of multicasting.

Multicast addresses are used by routing protocols such as EIGRP and OSPF, and IPv6 uses several for routing and device identification and auto-addressing features.

In IPv4, multicast addresses range from 224 to 239.

Class E addresses are reserved for experimental use only, so it is very unlikely you will ever use them. Addresses range from 240 to 255. I only mention this in case you are asked this in an exam or job interview.

Private Addresses

In order to help prevent wastage of IP addresses certain addresses were reserved for use on private networks. Any individual can use these addresses on their network provided they do not try to get out to the internet. The address allocation scheme was suggested in RFC* 1918, 'Address Allocation for Private Internets'.

> **IN THE REAL WORLD:** In order to get out to the internet a technique known as NAT (network address translation) is used to swap your private address to a public address.

The private (reserved) addresses are:

10.x.x.x – Any IP address beginning with 10
172.16.x.x – 172.31.x.x – Any IP starting with 172.16 to 172.31 inclusive
192.168.x.x – Any IP address starting with 192.168

This idea proved to be an ideal way to avoid wasting thousands of IP addresses. You will see reserved IP addresses used on most corporate networks as well as in homes. Below is the output for my home router. The router IP address is 192.168.0.1 and it allocates addresses to other hosts from the 192.168.0.x range.

Fig. 1.3—My home router information

RFC stands for request for comments. These are submitted documents suggesting how network protocols will work. You can read more at http://www.rfc-editor.org

SUMMARY

We can condense what we know so far to:

Class A – first bit set to 0, address range 1–126 (127 is reserved for testing) Network.Host.Host.Host

Class B – first bits set to 10, address range 128–191 Network.Network.Host.Host

Class C – first bits set to 110, address range 192–223 Network.Network.Network.Host

Class D – first bits set to 1110, address range 224–239

Class E – first bits set to 11110, address range 240–255

We only need to look at the number in the first octet to recognize which class address we are dealing with.

10.1.2.1 = Class A

190.2.3.4 = Class B

220.3.4.2 = Class C

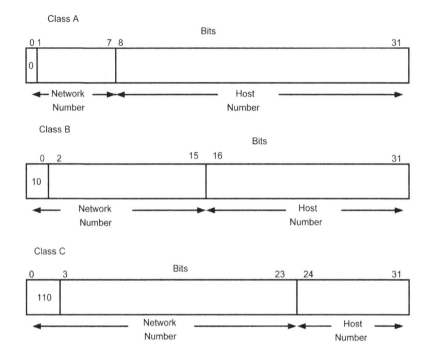

Fig. 1.4—Summary of Network Classes

You will observe in the above figure that bit counts start at zero, which can often confuse new IT students.

The private IP address ranges are:

10.0.0.0 – 10.255.255.255
172.16.0.0 – 172.31.255.255
192.168.0.0 – 192.168.255.255

There is another range of addresses known as Automatic Private IP Addressing. APIPA assigns a Class B IP address from 169.254.0.0 to 169.254.255.255 to a Windows client when a DHCP server is either permanently or temporarily unavailable.

Subnetting

Subnetting can be one of the most difficult subjects to master for many IT people. There is a long way to subnet and a very short and easy way. It is vital you understand how the long way works first, but then in real life you will use the short one (the easy way).

> **IN THE REAL WORLD**: You would need to use the longhand way of working out subnetting when designing an IP addressing scheme for a client. You would store the address range on a spreadsheet or a special type of software program used to track IP address allocation.

ADDRESS DEPLETION

Shortly after the IPv4 addressing scheme was implemented, it became apparent that there were not enough addresses to meet the demand. More and more organizations were using computers and networking equipment, and the current scheme was wasting thousands of addresses.

Example

A company is given a Class A address. Class A addresses can only be allocated to 126 companies. The first octet is used for the network, and the other three octets are free for use on the network.

If we use every combination of numbers in the remaining three octets (3 × 8), then we have a maximum value of over 16 million host addresses (specifically, 16,777,216). We can actually work out how many networks or hosts we have by using the powers of two.

> **FOR EXAMS**: You will have to be very familiar with the powers of two, hex, and binary to pass exams such as CCNA and Network+.

So we have three octets that are free for hosts on the network, giving us 3 times 8 bits, which equals 24.

2^{24}, that is, $2 \times 2 = 16{,}777{,}216$ hosts and 1 network

Don't worry about the math yet. I just want to illustrate the huge wastage involved in how IP addresses were first allocated and before steps were taken to try to extend the life of the IPv4 addressing method.

Historically, what happened was that a very large organization would be allocated a Class A address. They would need around 10,000 host addresses and waste the other 16 million plus. Because they owned the network number, it couldn't be shared with other organizations, so the other addresses were wasted.

For a Class B address the story was very similar. For Class B networks, the first two octets are reserved for the network address, which leaves two for host addressing. This gives us over 65,000 host addresses available per Class B IP address.

2^{16} is $2 \times 2 \times 2 \times 2 \times 2 \times 2 \times 2 \times 2 \times 2 \times 2 \times 2 \times 2 \times 2 \times 2 \times 2 \times 2 = 65{,}536$ hosts.

INSPIRATION: Working out IP addressing and subnetting can seem like learning another language at times. Confusion comes before inspiration, not the other way around.

HOW TO SUBNET

The problem with the initial way of using IP addresses was that we were fixed with having certain parts of the address for the network and certain parts for the hosts.

Class A addresses were fixed with 8 bits for the network and 24 for the hosts. Class B addresses were fixed with 16 bits for the network and 16 for the hosts. Class C addresses were fixed with 24 bits for the network and 8 for the hosts. There had to be some way for host addresses to be conserved. The answer came with the introduction of subnetting.

Subnetting allowed bits that were normally used for the host part to be used for the subnet part of the address. 'Subnetting' is short for 'subnetworking' and 'subnet' is short for 'subnetwork'. In order to let the routers or PCs know that subnetting was being used, another number had to be applied to the IP address. This number is known as the subnet mask and is also a binary value.

> **IN THE REAL WORLD**: Subnetting and many other internetworking methods and tools are introduced by requests for comments, or RFCs. RFCs are open for anybody to comment on before they are published: www.rfc-editor.org

Each bit on the subnet mask is compared with the bits on the IP address to determine which parts belong to the network and which belong to the host. A default subnet mask is allocated to each class of address. If you do not want to use subnetting, simply add the default subnet mask to the end of the IP address. It is not possible to enter an IP address onto a PC or router without also entering the subnet mask. Many actually fill the default value in for you once you enter the IP address.

Default subnet masks:

Class A – 255.0.0.0, or in binary:
11111111.00000000.00000000.00000000

Class B – 255.255.0.0, or in binary:
11111111.11111111.00000000.00000000

Class C – 255.255.255.0, or in binary:
11111111.11111111.11111111.00000000

We can see that the first octet for Class A addresses is reserved for the network number. This is the default anyway, like the first two octets for Class B and the first three for Class C.

A rule for subnet masks is that the 1 and 0 network and host bits must be contiguous—i.e., connect without a break. So you can have:

11111111.11111111.0000000.000000

But you cannot have:

11111111.000111111.00000000.00000000

We can also see how important it is to remember that the router or PC sees numbers in binary.

IN THE REAL WORLD: Whenever a network address does not look right to you, write it out in binary.

What we now have is a situation where each part of the IP address is matched with the subnet mask to determine which bits are part of the network identification and which bits are part of the host identification.

Example

10001100.10110011.11110000.11001000   140.179.240.200 Class B
11111111.11111111.00000000.00000000   255.255.0.0 Subnet mask

----

10001100.10110011.00000000.00000000 140.179.0.0 Network address

How did we get this number? The router performs a process known as logical ANDing. It compares the 1s and 0s to establish which numbers belong to the network and which belong to the host.

	0	1
0	0	0
1	0	1

So all the values are compared and everything apart from a 1 and a 1 equals 0. Check the above example again to make sure you understand how it works.

> **IN THE REAL WORLD**: Many network engineers do not understand subnetting. Make sure you are not one of them. Once you know it, you know it forever.

Because you now know which are the network addresses and which are the hosts, you can start assigning IP addresses to hosts on your network. If all the host bits are 0, then you cannot use this to put on a network host. The part with all 0s represents the subnet; we shall see why and how shortly.

140.179.0.0 is your network address.

140.179.0.0 has all of the host bits turned off:

10001100.10110011.00000000.00000000 ← Every host bit is turned off.
Network. Network. Host.   Host

If you want to start using host addresses on your network, you can simply start with number 1 and count up.

140.179.0.1 can be used for your first host.
140.179.0.2 can be used for your second host.

You can keep adding hosts until both the third and fourth octets are (almost) full.

140.179.0.255 is still a valid host number.
140.179.1.255 is still okay.
140.179.255.254 is the last host number you can use.

Here is the last host number in binary:

10001100.10110011.<u>11111111.11111110</u> ← **Not every host bit is turned on.**
Network. Network. Host.   Host

Why can't we use the last bit for a host? An IP address with all 1s in the host portion is reserved to tell the network that the packet is a broadcast packet. A broadcast packet is a packet that must be examined by all hosts on the network (or, more specifically, all of the hosts on this portion of the network—i.e., the subnet). The number below is a broadcast packet to every host on the 140.179 network.

140.179.255.255 in binary has all the host bits turned on:

10001100.10110011.<u>11111111.11111111</u> ← **Every host bit is turned on.**
Network. Network. Host.   Host

Broadcasts are normal on networks; however, too many can indicate you need to upgrade the network, or can signify a fault on a device, such as a failing network card on a server or PC.

So now we can see that we are not permitted to use all 0s for the hosts since this is the network and we cannot use all 1s because this is reserved for a broadcast. For every network or subnet, two of the available addresses can't be used for host or interface addresses. Armed with this information, we will be able to decide how many available hosts we have per network or subnet.

> **FOR EXAMS**: You may be tested thoroughly in the exam on subnetting and working out how many hosts there are per subnet and which is the subnet and broadcast address. You must be able to do this quickly or you will run out of time.

We will use the powers of two formula to work out how many hosts we get on our subnet. For now, we will simply raise 2 to the power of how many host bits we have and take away 2, one for the network of all 0s and one for the broadcast address of all 1s. Later, we will use the Subnetting Cheat Chart to get the answer in a few seconds.

For our example of 140.179.0.0 255.255.0.0 we can see that we have the last two octets free (0.0) to allocate to hosts on the network. That is two lots of 8 binary bits, giving us 16 host bits in total. Using longhand, you take the number 2 and double it 16 times: 2, 4, 8, 16, 32, etc.

The formula is $2^n - 2$:
$2^{16} - 2 = 65,534$

Do you think it would be practical to have one network with over 65,000 hosts? We cannot break this network down into smaller units, and if we have a broadcast on the network, each and every single host on the network will have to stop what it is doing to listen to the broadcast packet to see if it is the intended recipient.

Let's start subnetting and steal some bits from the host part of the address and make a subnetwork from those bits. I will write out the network address in longhand to make it easier to understand:

140.179.00000 000.00000000
[16 bits] [5 bits] [11 bits   ]
[network][subnet][host bits]

We have stolen 5 of the host bits to use them to make our subnet. The advantage is that we now have more than one subnet we can use and we have fewer wasted hosts per subnet. We can use the powers of two formula to work out how many subnets we have and how many hosts there are per subnet. We do not have to take 2 away for the subnets.

2^5 (or $2 \times 2 \times 2 \times 2 \times 2$) = 32 subnets each with
2^{11} (or $2 \times 2 \times 2 \times 2 \times 2 \times 2 \times 2 \times 2 \times 2 \times 2 \times 2$ - 2) = 2046 hosts per subnet

Why would we want to do this? You have fewer hosts using the bandwidth on your network segment. It is far easier to administer smaller subnets than to administer one huge network. Additionally, it is desirable to limit the number of broadcasts on a given subnet because each and every host on a subnet must examine the contents of a broadcast packet, whether it is the intended recipient or not.

In an environment with an excessive number of hosts, the number of broadcasts can grow quite a bit, and while not immediately measurable, this broadcast traffic will lower the overall performance of all of the networked systems. Also, you can have only one network per router interface. It is better to have a smaller number of hosts connected to a router interface than have several thousand.

Remember: the more host bits you steal, the more subnets you get, but each of those subnets is capable of supporting a lower number of hosts. Deciding how many hosts you need and how many hosts there are per subnet is part of the network design phase. The more host bits we steal, the more subnets and the fewer host bits become available; this is the trade-off.

Table 1.3 below shows the possible values for a Class B network. Remember that for Class B addresses we are looking at the third and fourth octets for the bit pattern. The first two octets are used for the network address and cannot be stolen. The CIDR column stands for Classless Inter-Domain Routing. This allows you to represent the subnet mask in bits instead of longhand, so /16 means there are 16 binary bits in the subnet mask, or 255.255.0.0. We will cover CIDR in more detail later.

Bit Pattern (3rd/4th Octet)	CIDR	Masked Bits	Subnets	Hosts Per Subnet ($2^n - 2$)
00000000.00000000	/16 255.255.0.0	0	1 (network)	65534
10000000.00000000	/17 255.255.128.0	1	2	32766
11000000.00000000	/18 255.255.192.0	2	4	16382
11100000.00000000	/19 255.255.224.0	3	8	8190
11110000.00000000	/20 255.255.240.0	4	16	4094
11111000.00000000	/21 255.255.248.0	5	32	2046
11111100.00000000	/22 255.255.252.0	6	64	1022
11111110.00000000	/23 255.255.254.0	7	128	510
11111111.00000000	/24 255.255.255.0	8	256	254
11111111.10000000	/25 255.255.255.128	9	512	126
11111111.11000000	/26 255.255.255.192	10	1024	62
11111111.11100000	/27 255.255.255.224	11	2048	30
11111111.11110000	/28 255.255.255.240	12	4096	14
11111111.11111000	/29 255.255.255.248	13	8192	6
11111111.11111100	/30 255.255.255.252	14	16384	2
11111111.11111110	/31 255.255.255.254	15	32768	0 (not usable)

Table 1.3—Class B subnetting summary

HOW TO WRITE OUT SUBNET MASKS

We do not write out the subnet mask bits in binary; we have a way of writing subnet masks when entering them on network equipment and when writing them out by hand.

If we steal 5 host bits from the third octet, we have to add the binary values together. Our Subnetting Cheat Chart will make this easier, but it's important we know where these numbers come from!

128	64	32	16	8	4	2	1
1	1	1	1	1	0	0	0

So we have 128 + 64 + 32 + 16 + 8 = 248.

Remember that we are using a Class B example here and so are working with the third octet. We are not allowed to alter the first two octets; they are fixed for the network.

255.255.248.0

This tells the router that we are subnetting and that we are using the first 5 host bits to carve out our subnets.

Things can get a little bit (more) complicated and we can no longer rely on what our eyes are telling us because the router is looking at a binary value and we are looking at a decimal value. Don't worry too much though because we will look at the quick and easy way to work out subnetting later.

In order for the router to know if a host is on a certain subnet, it looks to the masked bits. If all of the masked bits match, then it follows that the host must be on the same subnet. If the subnet bits do not match, then the hosts are on different subnets.

This time we have IP address 129.10.147.1 255.255.248.0.

Again we have a Class B address and are stealing 5 bits for subnetting. We know we have stolen 5 bits because 248 in binary is 11111000, which is 5 masked bits. Please work that out on paper now; we will use a cheat chart later for speed and accuracy.

10000001.00001010.<u>10010</u>011.00010000 129.10.147.32

10000001.00001010.<u>10010</u>100.01010101 129.10.148.85

We can see that the subnet bits in the example above both match, so the host addresses belong to the same subnet and you could safely use them for hosts. Now look at the below example:

10000001.00001010.<u>10011</u>010.00000010 129.10.154.2

This time one of the subnet bits has changed: the last value for the subnet is now 1 instead of 0. The router or PC can see it is a different subnet. Unfortunately, when we write it out in decimal, it is not very easy for us to see that this third IP address is in a different subnet. This is why learning subnetting can be problematic. It can look right but actually be wrong inasmuch as the hosts belong to different subnets.

Please read the above paragraph again. We have just encountered the reason why millions of IT students and engineers can't work out how to subnet!

CHANGING THE SUBNET REPRESENTATION

Although subnet masks are displayed as dotted decimals, the format can be changed on Cisco routers to bit count or hex with the 'ip netmask-format bit' command. Other vendors may offer this option but use a different command.

```
Router#show interface serial 0
Serial0 is administratively down, line protocol is down
 Hardware is HD64570
 Internet address is 192.168.1.1 255.255.255.0

RouterA#terminal ip netmask-format ?
RouterA#
 bit-count   Display netmask as number of significant bits
 decimal     Display netmask in dotted decimal
 hexadecimal Display netmask in hexadecimal

RouterA#terminal ip netmask-format bit-count

Router#show interface serial 0
Serial0 is administratively down, line protocol is down
 Hardware is HD64570
 Internet address is 192.168.1.1/24
```

'Bit-count' shows the address with a CIDR (slash value), such as 192.168.1.1/24. Decimal displays the subnet mask in dotted decimals, such as 255.255.255.0. Hex shows the mask in hex, such as 0Xffffff00.

As we have seen, there are only certain values available to use as a subnet mask due to binary mathematics. This is illustrated in Table 1.4 below.

Binary Value	Subnet Value
00000000	0
10000000	128
11000000	192
11100000	224
11110000	240
11111000	248
11111100	252
11111110	254
11111111	255

Table 1.4—Subnet mask values

If you calculate a subnet mask and it is some other value, such as 160, it is clearly wrong!

VARIABLE-LENGTH SUBNET MASKING (VLSM)

Although subnetting provides a useful mechanism to improve the IP addressing issue, network administrators were able to use only one subnet mask for an entire network. RFC 1009 addressed this issue by allowing a subnetted network to use more than one subnet mask. We have already seen examples of this in fact.

Now a network administrator could have a Class B address with a 255.255.192.0 mask but could further break that subnet down into smaller units with masks, such as 255.255.224.0. This would be the same as cutting a cake into four slices and taking one of those slices to make two (or more) smaller slices.

Using VLSM, we no longer need to worry about the class system for addressing networks. You can use a Class C subnet mask with a Class A network address, for example. So if you see 10.10.10.0 255.255.255.0, don't be surprised. We will use these examples later on in this book.

CLASSLESS INTER-DOMAIN ROUTING (CIDR)

RFC 1517, 1518, 1519, and 1520 specify CIDR features. CIDR is an extension of VLSM and it removed the need for classes of IP addresses and was yet another solution to the problem of depletion of IP addresses.

Instead of writing out the subnet in decimal, engineers in the real world use something called a slash address or CIDR. They write out how many bits are used for subnetting. If you are reading out such an address to a colleague, you will literally say 'slash', so for example, '192 dot 16 dot 8 dot 1 slash 24'.

I only mention this to prepare you for when you hear a colleague, customer, or other support engineer saying this. CIDR is used with ALL IPv6 addresses in fact because the concept of a subnet mask doesn't apply to these address types, so it's best you get used to it now.

Examples:

255.255.0.0 can be expressed as /16 because there are 16 binary bits used in the subnet mask:
11111111.11111111.00000000.00000000 = 16 on or masked bits

255.255.192.0 can be expressed as /18 because there are 18 binary bits masked:
11111111.11111111.11000000.00000000 = 18 on or masked bits

255.255.240.0 can be expressed as /20 because there are 20 binary bits masked:
11111111.11111111.11110000.00000000 = 20 on or masked bits

I'm sure you get the idea. We are no longer thinking about what class an IP address is anymore but what the CIDR value is. You still need to know how to write this out in full as a subnet mask because you could be asked to do this in an IT exam or job interview.

Also, many equipment vendors for routers, firewalls, and servers force you to write out the subnet mask in longhand but your design sheet may have the values in CIDR.

SUPERNETTING

CIDR allows for a feature known as route aggregation, whereby a single route in a routing table can represent several network addresses, saving bandwidth, router CPU cycles, and routing table size.

Route aggregation is also referred to as supernetting. Supernetting enables you to advertise a summary of your network addresses provided you have a contiguous block. For example, if you owned the networks 172.16.20.0/24 to 172.16.23.0/24, you could advertise just a single network of 172.16.20.0/22 out to the internet. The advantage is a saving on bandwidth and greater efficiency. This process is also known as route summarization or supernetting depending on who you are talking to or which vendor's notes you are reading.

Route summarization works only if you work out the addresses in binary first. Take the below four networks as a simple example:

11111111.11111111.11111111.00000000 = 24-bit mask
10101100.00010000.00010100.00000000 = 172.16.20.0
10101100.00010000.00010101.00000000 = 172.16.21.0
10101100.00010000.00010110.00000000 = 172.16.22.0
10101100.00010000.00010111.00000000 = 172.16.23.0

All of the bold parts of the address are common and can be aggregated with one subnet mask to advertise them all. There are 22 common bits, so we can use the mask 255.255.252.0 or /22 to advertise the entire block of addresses. You would usually use the lowest network number with the supernet value.

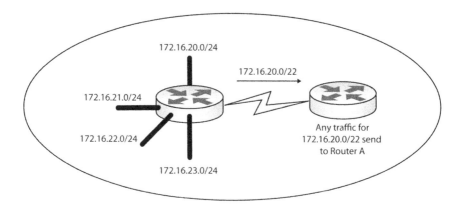

172.16.20.0/24

172.16.20.0/22

172.16.21.0/24

172.16.22.0/24

Any traffic for
172.16.20.0/22 send
to Router A

172.16.23.0/24

Fig. 1.5—Supernetting reduces the number of routes advertised

Now imagine you have 250 networks to advertise out to the internet or to a HQ router. You could supernet networks 172.16.0.0 to 172.16.250.0 inclusive as 172.16.0.0/16, saving a huge amount of resources on your network. This is why learning how to subnet is so useful to you in your IT career.

CIDR allows the use of the slash system for representing subnet masks—e.g., /26 instead of 255.255.255.192. Table 1.5 below is a Class C subnetting chart with CIDR representation.

Masked Bits	Subnet Mask	CIDR	Subnets	Hosts
0	255.255.255.0	/24	1 network	254
1	255.255.255.128	/25	2	126
2	255.255.255.192	/26	4	62
3	255.255.255.224	/27	8	30
4	255.255.255.240	/28	16	14
5	255.255.255.248	/29	32	6
6	255.255.255.252	/30	64	2

Table 1.5—CIDR

HOW MANY SUBNETS AND HOW MANY HOSTS?

Understanding this formula is crucial to passing IT exams such as CCNA and CompTIA Network+ and to real-life networking. Many networking emergencies could have been avoided by planning for future requirements during the design stage.

> **IN THE REAL WORLD**: When planning a network addressing scheme, always ask the client what their expected growth for the next few years is and account for that. Never design a network addressing scheme for just what they have now.

Given a network ID and subnet mask, how many subnets can we form, and how many hosts are there per subnet?

It all boils down to the powers of two (I told you knowing this would come in handy later).

255.255.224.0
11111111.11111111.11100000.00000000
[16 bits]   [3 bits] [13 bits]
[Network]   [Subnet] [Host]

So in the Class B example above we have 3 subnet bits to use and we can use every combination of three binary numbers to make up different subnets. I mention the fact it's Class B only so you know that the first two octets are reserved for the network already.

000,001,010,101,011,110,100,111

This gives us eight subnets to use. Alternatively we could say:

$2^3 (2 \times 2 \times 2) = 8$

The total number of subnets will always be 2 to the power of subnet bits.

How many hosts?

We have 13 bits left for the host addresses.

2^{13} - 2 = 8190

So for this subnet mask we can see we have eight subnets and each subnet has 8190 hosts available for use.

I know this seems somewhat long-winded, but I want to ensure you know how and why this is all happening before you move into the fast way. You need to know in case you are asked by your customer to explain or in a technical IT job interview when they wonder how you got the answer so quickly!

INSPIRATION: Don't worry if none of this makes any sense at the moment. Just keep on going. Once you learn the easy way to subnet using the Subnetting Cheat Chart you will realize that this is not difficult at all.

Example

What are the host addresses and broadcast address for the below subnet?

131.107.32.0 (Network Address)
255.255.224.0 (Subnet Mask)

We have a Class B address and are taking 3 bits from the host bits (3 binary bits is 11100000, which is 128 + 64 + 32, or 224). There isn't room to fit in every permutation, so we have had to shorten the output and skip a lot of host addresses (indicated by 'keep going' below).

11111111.11111111.11100000.00000000 255.255.224.0 subnet mask
10000011.01101011.00100000.00000000 131.107.32.0* (this is the subnet)
10000011.01101011.00100000.00000001 131.107.32.1 (this is the first host)
10000011.01101011.00100000.00000010 131.107.32.2 (this is the second host)
10000011.01101011.00100000.00000011 131.107.32.3 (this is the third host)
10000011.01101011.00100001.11111111 131.107.33.255 (we keep counting up)
10000011.01101011.00100011.11111111 131.107.35.255 (keep going)
10000011.01101011.00100111.11111110 131.107.39.254 (keep going)

10000011.01101011.00111111.11111110 131.107.63.254 (this is the last host)
10000011.01101011.00111111.11111111 131.107.63.255* (the broadcast address)

So our hosts are 131.107.32.1 to 131.107.63.254 (8190 in total).

*131.107.32.0 = subnet and 131.107.63.255 = broadcast address

Because the IP address changed from 32.1 to 33.255 and all the way up to 63.254, it is easy to look at it and mistake them for different subnets. When we write out the addresses correctly, we can see that all of the hosts above are on the same subnet.

In the above example, the first subnet would be 131.107.0.0, which we refer to as the zero subnet. We will look at this in more detail shortly. For now I just want you to follow along with my examples.

All the hosts on the same subnet (for example, the 131.107.32.0 subnet) will have to be attached to one router interface or be in the same VLAN. You cannot decide to put half of your addresses on one side of the router and half on the other. Many engineers have made this mistake and wasted hours trying to troubleshoot the problem.

INSPIRATION: It may take several reviews of this book to understand IP addressing and subnetting. There is no need to get disheartened if it doesn't sink in the first time or even the tenth time; just keep following the examples and re-reading.

SUBNET ZERO

There used to be a rule that you couldn't use the first and last subnet numbers when subnetting. This was called the subnet zero rule. This has long been removed but I just wanted to mention it in case another IT engineer bring it up. You CAN use the first and last available subnet now and we do throughout this book.

SHORTCUT METHOD

Writing out IP addresses and subnets in binary is very time consuming. There is an easier way to do it. Just follow five simple steps. Once we go through this shortcut method a few times, we will move on to an even easier subnetting method using the Subnetting Cheat Chart.

If we skipped to the cheat method first, you could already answer subnetting questions, but you wouldn't actually understand what is happening behind the scenes, which would make you a substandard network engineer and we can't have that, can we?

Step 1. How many subnets?
2 to the power of masked bits or 2^n

Step 2. How many hosts per subnet?
2 to the power of unmasked bits minus 2 (shown as -2)

Step 3. What are the valid subnets?
256 – the rightmost non-zero subnet to give us the subnet increment

Step 4. What are the valid hosts per subnet?

Step 5. What is the broadcast address of the subnet?

Example

Which subnet is 131.107.32.1 255.255.224.0 in?

255.255.224.0 is 11111111.11111111.<u>111</u>00000.00000000 in binary.

We could actually write this out with a slash mask of /19 (19 masked network bits or 1s). You can see that we are subnetting in the third octet here (and of course 131 is Class B, so the first two octets are fixed for network bits).

1. How many subnets?

We have stolen 3 bits (128 + 64 + 32 = 224 subnet), so:
$2^3 = 8$ subnets (or $2 \times 2 \times 2 = 8$)

2. How many hosts per subnet?

We have 13 bits left for hosts, so:
$2^{13} - 2 = 8190$ (or double the number two 13 times, then subtract 2)

3. What are the valid subnets?

Take the rightmost non-zero subnet (224) away from 256:
$256 - 224 = 32$

We now know that we have eight valid subnets and each subnet will be an increment of 32. We can start at 0 for the first subnet, so 0, 32, 64, 96, 128,160,192, and 224. 224 is also permitted.

This part is crucial. If you get it wrong, then all of your subnetting will be off, so double-check it. Some people make the mistake of doubling the numbers—i.e., 32, 64, 128, etc.

4. What are the valid hosts per subnet?

It is best to write out the subnet number and the next subnet number. From this we can work out our first and last valid hosts. We can actually see that our host is in the second subnet, but I'll keep on counting so you understand the process. In any exam you take, please stop as soon as you get the answer of course.

1st Subnet 131.107.0.0 ← **This is the zero subnet.**
2nd Subnet 131.107.32.0 ← **131.107.32.1 is in this subnet.**
3rd Subnet 131.107.64.0
4th Subnet 131.107.96.0
5th Subnet 131.107.128.0
6th Subnet 131.107.160.0

7th Subnet 131.107.192.0
8th Subnet 131.107.224.0

So now we know we can use any number, including the 224 subnet. It is fairly clear from the list above that the host address we are looking for is on the second subnet (where I put ←), so we can look at the available host numbers on this. The host numbers are everything after the subnet value and before the broadcast address.

Subnet - 131.107.32.0
1st Host - 131.107.32.1
2nd Host - 131.107.32.2
3rd host - 131.107.32.3...We could keep going but there are over 8000 hosts.
Last host - 131.107.63.254 (take 1 away from the broadcast to get this value)
Broadcast - 131.107.63.255 (take 1 away from the next subnet to get this value!)

For the third or .64 subnet we follow the same process of writing out the subnet and broadcast address. We can work out the broadcast address by writing out the next subnet address and taking 1 away. The subnet starting 131.107.64 is the third of our eight subnets. We then take 1 away from that to determine the broadcast address for the previous subnet.

Subnet - 131.107.64.0 (take 1 away to get the broadcast for the .32 subnet)
1st host - 131.107.64.1
Last host - 131.107.95.254
Broadcast - 131.107.95.255

We could go on, but can you see that we have gone past the IP address we are trying to find, which is 131.107.32.1?

5. What is the broadcast address?

Broadcast address - 131.107.63.255

It is pretty easy to work out if you write out the subnets first.

So what just happened here?

Without being able to see the whole thing in binary it does look a little strange. You just have to have confidence that the method works, and if in doubt, go back to binary. We can prove that the broadcast address is such by checking to see if it is all 1s in binary. The last host will be the last number we can use without having all 1s (255 in decimal).

10000011.01101011.<u>001</u>11111.11111110 131.107.63.254 (One host bit not on)
10000011.01101011.<u>001</u>11111.11111111 131.107.63.255 (All host bits are on here)

The underlined bits are the subnet bits. The .254 subnet has all the bits apart from 1 turned on. The broadcast address has all the host bits turned on. This tells the network that it is a broadcast packet to the subnet.

If we follow the process for each subnet using a subnet of 255.255.224.0 going up in increments of 32, we will get the following host numbers:

Subnet 1: 131.107.0.1 to 131.107.31.254
Subnet 2: 131.107.32.1 to 131.107.63.254 ← **131.107.32.1 is in this subnet.**
Subnet 3: 131.107.64.1 to 131.107.95.254
Subnet 4: 131.107.96.1 to 131.107.127.254
Subnet 5: 131.107.128.1 to 131.107.159.254
Subnet 6: 131.107.160.1 to 131.107.191.254
Subnet 7: 131.107.192.1 to 131.107.223.254
Subnet 8: 131.107.224.1 to 131.107.255.254

You already know by now I'm sure, but each octet starts at 0 and rolls up to the maximum value of 255. As it rolls up, the left one can count up by 1. If I write this out in decimal:

1.255 – We add 1 to the last octet, which gives us:

2.0

And of course it goes backwards, so this is how you work out the broadcast address from the next subnet. I'll write out a broadcast address, but I got it from rolling back the next subnet address by 1. We'll presume the subnets are going up in increments of 32.

192.168.1.31 – broadcast address for the 192.168.1.0 subnet
192.168.1.32 – subnet address

INSPIRATION: If you still don't understand any of this, be assured that this is perfectly normal. Remember your first driving lesson?

Example

Which subnet is host 10.20.1.23 255.240.0.0 in?

We have taken 4 bits from the second octet (240 in binary is 11110000 or bits turned on in the 128 + 64 + 32 + 16 columns) to make subnets. Class A addresses normally have the default 8 bits (255.0.0.0 is 11111111.0000 000.0000000.00000000 in binary), which is how you determine that 4 bits have been used.

1. How many subnets?

$2^4 = 16$

2. How many hosts per subnet?

We have 20 bits left for hosts, so:

$2^{20} - 2 = 1,048,574$ hosts per subnet

3. What are the valid subnets?

256 - 240 = 16 (the increment). Our subnets go up in increments of 16.

10.0.0.0 (the zero subnet)
10.16.0.0 ← **10.20.1.23 is in this subnet.**
10.32.0.0
10.48.0.0…all the way up to
10.224.0.0
10.240.0.0

4. What are the valid hosts per subnet?

10.0.0.0: Hosts 10.0.0.1 to 10.15.255.254
10.16.0.0: Hosts 10.16.0.1 to 10.31.255.254
10.32.0.0: Hosts 10.32.0.1 to 10.47.255.254
10.48.0.0: Hosts 10.48.0.1 to 10.63.255.254
10.64.0.0 and so on
10.224.0.0: Hosts 10.224.0.1 to 10.239.255.254
10.240.0.1: Hosts 10.240.0.1 to 10.255.255.254

5. What are the broadcast addresses?

This is the last address before each subnet.

10.15.255.254 is the last host on the first subnet.
10.15.255.255 is the broadcast address.

10.16.0.0 is the next subnet.
10.16.0.1 is the first host on the next subnet.
10.31.255.254 is the last host.
10.31.255.255 is the broadcast address.

10.32.0.0 is the next subnet.
10.47.255.255 is the broadcast on the third subnet.

10.48.0.0 is the next subnet, etc.

You will learn how to reduce these steps shortly.

Note also that I'm continuing past the step where we found the answer, which was back in Step 3. I'm teaching you how to subnet before we drill down to just answering exam questions.

EXAM QUESTIONS

In IT exams you will often have one of two types of subnetting questions. The first type you have just seen. You are given a certain network number and subnet mask and you need to determine which subnet the IP address is in. The second type of question is to design a subnet mask to give a customer a certain number of hosts and a certain number of subnets.

The Subnetting Cheat Chart will answer both types very quickly, but we will cover the longer methods first so you can see how the binary math works behind the scenes.

We will now shorten the previous five steps. It does help though to go through them to answer any type of subnetting question.

Example

Which subnet is host 192.168.21.41/28 in?

The first task is to work out how to change the /28 mask into a full subnet mask. You already know that each octet is 8 binary bits, and 8 + 8 + 8 = 24 binary bits, which is 255.255.255.0. We need to add 4 to 24 to get 28, which is 128 + 64 + 32 + 16 binary places or 11110000 or 240.

With 4 bits of masking we know we have 2^4 = 16 subnets. This leaves 4 bits for the hosts, which is 2^4 - 2 = 14 hosts per subnet.

The subnet mask is 255.255.255.240 (4 masked bits in the last octet):

256 - 240 = 16 increment.

We want to go up in subnet increments of 16 (starting at 0) until we find the one where host 41 is (subnet 3 below).

Subnet 1: 192.168.21.0, hosts 1-14 (broadcast = 15)
Subnet 2: 192.168.21.16, hosts 17-30 (broadcast = 31)
Subnet 3: 192.168.21.32, hosts 33-46* (broadcast = 47) ← **41 here.**
Subnet 4: 192.168.21.48, hosts 49-62 (broadcast = 63)
Subnet 5: 192.168.21.64, hosts 65-78 (broadcast = 79)
and so on...up to
Subnet 16: 192.168.21.240, hosts 241-254 (broadcast = 255)

Example

Which subnet is host 10.65.2.5/10 in?

Turn /10 into a subnet mask. 255 is 8 binary bits, so we need to add 2 to get to 10 and 2 binary bits is 128 + 64, which is 192 or 11000000.

2 masked subnet bits = 255.192.0.0, so 2^2 = 4 subnets. We have 2^{22} - 2 = 4,194,302 hosts per subnet.

256 - 192 = 64 increment

Subnet 1: 10.0.0.0, hosts 10.0.0.1 – 10.63.255.254 (broadcast = 255)
Subnet 2: 10.64.0.0, hosts 10.64.0.1 – 10.127.255.254 ← **10.65.2.5 is in here.** (broadcast = 255)
Subnet 3: 10.128.0.0, hosts 10.128.0.1 – 10.191.255.254 (broadcast = 255)
Subnet 4: 10.192.0.0, hosts 10.192.0.1 – 10.255.255.254 (broadcast = 255)

Let's use the Subnetting Cheat Chart to answer the next question.

SUBNETTING CHEAT CHART

I'm about to solve all your subnetting problems. You can use this cheat chart in any IT exam or at work to quickly troubleshoot IP addressing issues and work out design projects for customers.

It's worth noting that in IT exams you are usually given an A4-sized whiteboard and marker pen. You can use these to write out the below chart and then refer to it to answer any subnetting problem. Just rub out the ticks and use it over and over. I've used it for my CompTIA Network+, CCNA, CCNP, and MCSE exams.

I devised the Subnetting Cheat Chart while I was preparing to teach my first CCNA classroom course in 2002. I just stumbled across it, to be totally honest. I started to see patterns in the subnetting questions I was writing and realized that you could write a simple chart to represent everything.

	Bits	128	64	32	16	8	4	2	1
Subnets									
128									
192									
224									
240									
248									
252									
254									
255									
Powers of Two	Subnets	Hosts Minus 2							
2									
4									
8									
16									
32									
64									
128									
256									
512									
1024									
2048									
4096									

Table 1.6—The Subnetting Cheat Chart

This chart formed the basis of a best-selling Amazon subnetting book and a video training course which have been used by many thousands of students over the last 16 years.

I still see people trying to teach subnetting in classrooms and on YouTube with a method that is usually far too tricky to remember or takes too long when it comes to answering exam questions.

Let's break the chart down into two and three components. The upper half is used to answer any 'which subnet is host X in?' question or similar ones. It could be 'what is the broadcast address for subnet X?' or 'which of the following hosts belong to subnet X?' It's all the same thing as far as the top portion is concerned.

The bottom half is to answer design-style questions. These are 'how many hosts / subnets per host' type questions, where you have to work out how many of each value a certain subnet mask or CIDR value gives you.

The very top row I'm sure you've already noticed is purely an octet—i.e., eight binary places. We use this for the octet we are subnetting in. If we have to subnet in two octets, we just use this for the last octet. We just add a '+8' in the top leftmost box. You will see how this works later.

If you use 4 bits for subnetting, you will tick four places in the Bits row. This gives you your subnet increment, which in this example would be 16. You start with the zero subnet and then count up in 16s. You would usually stop when you get to the subnet AFTER the one you find the host in.

	Bits	128	64	32	16	8	4	2	1

Next is the top left column. This represents the subnet value. If you were told that the subnet mask applied to a Class C network was /27, and wanted to know what it was in longhand, you would tick down three places. /24 is the default, and to get to /27 you need three.

Subnets
128
192
224
240
248
252
254
255

You would do this as a sanity check to avoid making mistakes in the exam or if you are rushed at work with a troubleshooting issue but want to ensure you are accurate.

Finally, the bottom half contains two columns. These represent the powers of two. How many host bits you steal you tick down the Subnets column. How many host bits are left you tick down the Hosts - 2 column.

If you had the mask /28 applied to a Class C network, you know 4 bits are stolen for use in subnetting, leaving 4 bits for hosts. Ticking down four in each column would give you 16 subnets, and each subnet would have 14 hosts.

Powers of Two	Subnets	Hosts -2
2		
4		
8		
16		
32		
64		
128		
256		
512		
1024		
2048		
4096		
8192		
16384		

For this part of the Subnetting Cheat Chart, you start with the number 2 and just keep doubling it. I tend to stop at 16,384 to save time. If you need to tick down more than 14 places, then just keep doubling the value. It would be pretty unfair in any exam for them to get you ticking down 20 or more places.

As with any tool, the more you use it, the easier the task becomes, so let's do some examples. From now on we will just refer to the Subnetting Cheat Chart to answer all questions. If you had to explain your working out in an interview or to a customer, you could revert to the slow method.

Example

Which subnet is 192.168.100.203/27 in?

This is a Class C network address. We know that three binary octets (24 bits) are the default mask for this network and to get to 27 we need to add 3. Tick down three numbers in the top subnetting column in the chart. This will give you the value of 224. So our subnet /27 is 255.255.255.224. We can then tick three (the same value) across the top to get the subnet increment, which is 32 (or just take 224 away from 256 if you prefer).

These ticks represent how many bits we have stolen to create subnetworks. In this example it's three. We don't need to use the bottom section of the chart because we aren't trying to figure out how many subnets and hosts per subnet there are.

	Bits	128	64	32	16	8	4	2	1
Subnets		✓	✓	✓					
128	✓								
192	✓								
224	✓								
240									
248									
252									
254									
255									
Powers of Two	Subnets	Hosts Minus 2							
2									
4									
8									
16									
32									
64									
128									
256									
512									
1024									
2048									
4096									
8192									
16384									

We are subnetting in the fourth octet, so we just count up in increments of 32 until we get to the one with the host number 203.

I usually prefer to jump the count in a multiple of 32 (160, for example) to save time, but you may prefer to start with 0, 32, 64, etc., for now. Just remember that in the exam, time is of the essence. Skipping up in higher values than the subnet increment I refer to as a 'jump strategy'. It won't matter too much if your increment is 128, 64, or even 32, but imagine trying to find host 209 when you are counting up in increments of 2 or 4!

Let's count up in increments of 32. Remember that we are looking for host number 203. You would typically count up to the next subnet after the one you think the host number is in just to make sure. Again, this is especially important if you are counting up in small increments, where it's easy to make mistakes.

Another reason to do this is you may be asked to work out the broadcast address for your subnet. The way to do this is to find the next subnet value and then subtract 1. For subnet 1 below, for example, the broadcast address is 31, which is the next subnet value minus 1.

Subnet 1: 192.168.100.0, hosts 1-30 (broadcast = 31)
Subnet 2: 192.168.100.32, hosts 33-62 (broadcast = 63)
Subnet 3: 192.168.100.64, hosts 65-94 (broadcast = 95)
Subnet 4: 192.168.100.96, hosts 97-126 (broadcast = 127)
Subnet 5: 192.168.100.128, hosts 129-158 (broadcast = 159)
Subnet 6: 192.168.100.160, hosts 161-190 (broadcast = 191)
Subnet 7: 192.168.100.192, hosts 193-222 (broadcast = 223) ← **203 is in here.**
Subnet 8: 192.168.100.224, hosts 225-254 (broadcast = 255)

The host 192.168.100.203 is in subnet 192.168.100.192.

In an IT exam you will be shown four or five choices, and one of these will be correct of course.

We will work through a lot more subnetting examples, but I wanted to briefly show you how the bottom half of the Subnetting Cheat Chart works. Before we do that, let's take another look at the entire chart.

Working Out How Many Hosts and How Many Subnets

	Bits	128	64	32	16	8	4	2	1
Subnets									
128									
192									
224									
240									
248									
252									
254									
255									
Powers of Two	Subnets	Hosts Minus 2							
2									
4									
8									
16									
32									
64									
128									
256									
512									
1024									
2048									
4096									

What the Subnetting Cheat Chart helps you to do is to easily and quickly work out how many bits are being used for subnetting, which subnet the host is on, how many hosts there are per subnet, and how many subnets there are.

Example

How many subnets and hosts does the network and mask 192.168.2.0/26 give us?

We are taking an extra 2 bits from the normal 24-bit mask. Tick off two numbers down in the left-hand Subnets column (128 and then 192), which gives us a mask of 192 or to be more specific 255.255.255.192. You don't actually have to do this step because they aren't asking you to write the subnet mask out in full in this question, but I wanted to show you how the chart works in full.

You can work out that it is 2 bits being used if you remember that each octet count is 8. 255.0.0.0 is 8 binary bits, 255.255.0.0 is 16, and 255.255.255.0 is 24. If we have a /26 mask, then we need to add 2 onto the 255.255.255.0 mask, which is 24 bits plus 2 more or 255.255.255.192.

We have taken 2 bits for the subnets, so in the Powers of Two column on the bottom left tick down two places (2 and then 4). This gives us four subnets. This would usually be your first step for any design-type question (such as this one).

Now we know we have 6 bits left for the hosts (8 - 2 = 6 bits remaining), so tick down six places in the Powers of Two column to get our number of hosts per subnet. Six down gives us 64, and taking 2 away for the subnet and broadcast gives us 62 hosts per subnet. Easy, isn't it?

Our answer then is that 192.168.2.0/26 gives us four subnets and each subnet has 62 host addresses available. We don't need to list the available subnets because we weren't asked to for this question.

Here is the Subnetting Cheat Chart with ticks applied.

	Bits	128	64	32	16	8	4	2	1
Subnets									
128	✓								
192	✓								
224									
240									
248									
252									
254									
255									
Powers of Two	Subnets	Hosts Minus 2							
2	✓	✓							
4	✓	✓							
8		✓							
16		✓							
32		✓							
64		✓							
128									
256									
512									
1024									
2048									
4096									
8192									
16384									

Subnetting Cheat Chart

Example

You are given an IP address of 192.168.5.0 255.255.255.0. You are the network administrator and need to subnet this address to make eight subnets each with 30 hosts.

Go back to the chart and tick down the powers of two until you get to a number that gives you the eight subnets. Two and four won't be enough, but eight is perfect. So now we know we need to steal 3 bits for subnetting. Tick down three places in the top Subnets column (starting at 128, then 192) and we get 224.

Stealing 3 bits leaves us 5 bits for hosts per subnet. If you tick down five places in the hosts per subnet column, you will see that this gives us 30 (32 - 2) hosts per subnet, which is enough for our requirements.

The answer is you need subnet 255.255.255.224 (or a /27 mask) to get your eight subnets. If you tick down three in the lower Subnets column, you can tick down three in the upper Subnets column to determine the correct subnet mask.

	Bits	128	64	32	16	8	4	2	1
Subnets									
128	✓								
192	✓								
224	✓								
240									
248									
252									
254									
255									
Powers of Two	Subnets	Hosts Minus 2							
2	✓	✓							
4	✓	✓							
8	✓	✓							
16		✓							
32		✓							
64									
128									
256									
512									
1024									
2048									
4096									
8192									
16384									

Subnetting Cheat Chart

Part 1 is the foundation we will build on in Part 2. You know now how subnets are built, how binary math works, what the address classes are, and how to subnet and work out how many subnets and hosts there are.

In Part 2 we will streamline the entire process so you can answer exam and technical interview questions in a rapid-fire format.

ANSWER THESE QUESTIONS

1. Write out 224 in binary.
2. How does a Class B address begin in binary?
3. What is the range for Class C addresses?
4. What are the reserved IP addresses?
5. Write out 255.255.255.252 as a slash address.
6. What subnet is host 192.168.2.130/26 in?
7. Which Class C subnet will allow for only two hosts?
8. The hex value C7 is what in decimal and binary?
9. An IPv6 address consists of how many bits?
10. What are Class D addresses used for?

Answers

1. 11100000
2. 10
3. 192-223
4. 10.x.x.x, 172.16.x.x-172.31.x.x, 192.168.x.x
5. /30
6. 192.168.2.128
7. 255.255.255.252
8. 199 and 11000111
9. IPv6 uses eight 16-bit hexadecimal number fields representing a 128-bit address.
10. Multicasting

The Subnetting Cheat Chart

	Bits	128	64	32	16	8	4	2	1
Subnets									
128	✓								
192	✓								
224	✓								
240									
248									
252									
254									
255									
Powers of Two	Subnets	Hosts Minus 2							
2	✓	✓							
4	✓	✓							
8	✓	✓							
16		✓							
32		✓							
64									
128									
256									
512									
1024									
2048									
4096									
8192									
16384									

Subnetting Cheat Chart

Part 2

In Part 2 we will review everything we already know to reinforce the knowledge, and then I'll start blitzing you with subnetting questions.

Sound like fun? You bet.

The Easy Way to Subnet

Subnetting is easy—really easy, in fact. You just need to treat it like a process, so follow my examples and keep going until it all sinks in.

By the end of this guide you will be well on your way to being able to answer most subnetting questions in your head in seconds. Make sure you have read through Part 1 before you launch into this part of the book. I am presuming you have read through that at least once and understood some of the fundamentals, such as the powers of two and binary mathematics.

I know I keep telling you this, but just relax and enjoy the learning process. Some of you will pick this up on the first read, but for the rest of us we have to keep rereading until we get some light-bulb moments. Just remember that I had to invent this entire process after failing my CCNA exam!

> **FOR THE EXAM**: When you reach the subnetting questions in the exam, RELAX! Take three deep breaths to get some extra oxygen into your brain, and just follow the steps you have learned here.

CLASS C SUBNETTING

Here are the possible Class C subnets:

Bits	Subnet Mask	CIDR	Subnets	Hosts
0	255.255.255.0	/24	1 network	254
1	255.255.255.128	/25	2	126
2	255.255.255.192	/26	4	62
3	255.255.255.224	/27	8	30
4	255.255.255.240	/28	16	14
5	255.255.255.248	/29	32	6
6	255.255.255.252	/30	64	2

Table 2.1—All possible Class C subnets

Logic tells us that the more host bits we steal, the more subnets we have but the fewer hosts we have available per subnet. As you see the number of subnets increase, you will see the hosts-per-subnet value decrease.

We know from Part 1 that if we subnet the longhand way, we need to follow five simple steps in order to answer any subnetting question. The five steps are as follows:

1. How many subnets?
2 to the power of masked bits

2. How many hosts per subnet?
2 to the power of unmasked bits - 2

3. What are the valid subnets?
256, the rightmost non-zero subnet

4. What are the valid hosts per subnet?

5. What is the broadcast address of the subnet?

The first subnet of a Class C address we can use involves taking 1 bit from the available 8 host bits. If you aren't sure of what is happening with the binary numbers, then go back to Part 1. For the quick method we won't have time to write things down in binary.

Important Note:

In all the following examples I show you how to determine which subnet a host is in as well as how many subnets and hosts per subnet are generated. It's important to remember that in any exam or interview, just answer the question you are given. Don't spend extra time working out how many hosts and subnets there are if you are asked only which subnet a host is in. It's wasted time.

My other book *101 Labs – IP Subnetting* does this all the way through— just getting to the answer without any messing around.

Example

Host 192.168.1.200 255.255.255.128 (or /25)

I know we are not supposed to have 1 bit for subnetting, but there are exceptions. It is slightly awkward to start with an exception, but we need to address it and there is no time like the present. You would use this subnet if you wanted two subnets each containing 126 hosts on a Class C subnet.

The Subnetting Cheat Chart works for this example. We can use the zero subnet, which is the first bit off, and the second subnet, which is the first bit on. I'll present the answer in table format for now to make it easy on your eyes.

Subnet	0	128
First host	1	129
Last host	126	254
Broadcast	127	255

We have taken 1 bit to use for the subnets, so tick down one place in the top Subnets column, which gives us the value 128 and in turn the subnet mask 255.255.255.128 (which would be useful if you had only been given the /25 mask i.e. in CIDR).

You then tick one place across the Bits row to reveal the increment our subnets go up in, which in this instance is 128. We can use the zero subnet, so our two subnet values end in 0 and 128.

	Bits	128	64	32	16	8	4	2	1
Subnets		✓							
128	✓								
192									
224									
240									
248									
252									
254									
255									
Powers of Two	Subnets	Hosts Minus 2							
2	✓	✓							
4		✓							
8		✓							
16		✓							
32		✓							
64		✓							
128		✓							
256									
512									
1024									
2048									
4096									
8192									
16384									

Subnet 1: 192.168.1.0, hosts 1-126 (broadcast 127)
Subnet 2: 192.168.1.128, hosts 129-254 (broadcast 255) ← **host 200 here**

The full answer then is 192.168.1.200/25 is in subnet 192.168.1.128.

If you were asking how many subnets and hosts per subnet there are, you would then tick one place down in the lower Subnets column to show that we have two subnets. We have 7 bits left for the hosts, so tick down seven places in the Hosts - 2 column to reveal that we have 126 (128 - 2) hosts per subnet.

If the above example doesn't make sense at the moment, then leave it for now and come back to it later. It will still be here and will make more sense after you go through the examples below.

Example

255.255.255.192 or /26

I've left off the host number for now because I want to ensure we know how to use the chart first. In this example we will cover a few possible questions. In reality it will more likely be just one aspect of the following which will form an exam question.

1. How many subnets?

We know that the default Class C mask is 24 bits or 255.255.255.0 and that this example is using a /26 mask, which means 2 bits have been stolen after the default mask. We can tick two boxes down the top Subnets column of the Subnetting Cheat Chart to get to the 192 box to determine the subnet mask value of 255.255.255.192 (you would need to do this if they only gave you the CIDR value).

Next, we can tick down two boxes in the Subnets column, giving us four subnets

$2^2 = 4$

So we have four subnets.

	Bits	128	64	32	16	8	4	2	1
Subnets		✓	✓						
128	✓								
192	✓								
224									
240									
248									
252									
254									
255									
Powers of Two	Subnets	Hosts Minus 2							
2	✓	✓							
4	✓	✓							
8		✓							
16		✓							
32		✓							
64		✓							
128									
256									
512									
1024									
2048									
4096									
8192									
16384									

2. How many hosts per subnet?

We have 6 bits in the octet left unchecked, so we know we have 6 bits left for the hosts column. We can now tick down six host boxes in the Powers of 2 column to get 64 minus 2. We have put the two columns together in the chart in order to save space and help you count.

$2^6 - 2 = 62$

3. What are the valid subnets?

We tick two places across the top Bits row because we ticked down two in the Subnets column. We count up in increments of 64. We start at zero and stop when we hit the subnet value (192).

0, 64, 128, 192. So each subnet number would end in:

x.x.x.0
x.x.x.64
x.x.x.128
x.x.x.192

4. What are the valid hosts per subnet / broadcast address?

We can actually answer questions four and five at the same time.

Subnet	0	64	128	192
First host	1	65	129	193
Last host	62	126	190	254
Broadcast	63	127	191	255

That was fairly simple, wasn't it? If you follow the Subnetting Cheat Chart, you can't go wrong.

If you are asked in the exam which subnet host 192.16.150.76/26 is in, you will see that it is within subnet 192.16.150.64 because 192.16.150.0 is too low and 192.16.150.128 is too high. The subnets will be:

Subnet 1 = 192.16.150.0, hosts 1-62 (broadcast 63)
Subnet 2 = 192.16.150.64, hosts 65-126 (broadcast 127) ← **host 76 here**
Subnet 3 = 192.16.150.128, hosts 129-190 (broadcast 191)
Subnet 4 = 192.16.150.192, hosts 193-254 (broadcast 255)

Example

Which subnet is host 200.100.206.99/27 in?

We have taken 1 more bit for subnetting as compared to the previous example. You know that getting to /24 requires a subnet mask of 255.255.255.0—i.e., 24 binary bits. We need to add 3 to 24 to get to 27, so now you have to tick down 3 bits from the top Subnets column to get 224. The subnet mask for /27 is therefore 255.255.255.224.

I'll also cover how to work out how many subnets and hosts per subnet there are, but this question didn't ask us to answer that. I just want to give you as much exposure as possible to this way of working out subnetting problems.

1. How many subnets?

$2^3 = 8$

Tick down three boxes in the lower Subnets column, which gives us eight subnets.

	Bits	128	64	32	16	8	4	2	1
Subnets		✓	✓	✓					
128	✓								
192	✓								
224	✓								
240									
248									
252									
254									
255									
Powers of Two	Subnets	Hosts Minus 2							
2	✓	✓							
4	✓	✓							
8	✓	✓							
16		✓							
32		✓							
64									
128									
256									
512									
1024									

2. How many hosts per subnet?

We have 5 remaining bits for the hosts. Tick down five places in the Powers of 2 column to get 32, and take away 2.

$2^5 - 2 = 30$

So we have eight subnets, each with 30 hosts.

3. What are the valid subnets?

We take 224 away from 256, or (better still) tick three across the top Bits row. This gives us the subnet increment.

256 - 224 = 32

0, 32, 64, 96, 128, 160, 192, 224

So our subnets are going up in increments of 32.

4. What are the valid hosts per subnet / broadcast address?

Subnet	0	32	64	96	128	160	192	224
First host	1	33	65	97	129	161	193	225
Last host	30	62	94	126	158	190	222	254
Broadcast	31	63	95	127	159	191	223	255

The above boxes represent the last octet, so if you wanted to write the subnets out in full, you would have:

200.100.206.0
200.100.206.32
200.100.206.64 (we still haven't reached the .99 host)
200.100.206.96 ← **host 99 here**
200.100.206.128 (we have the answer, so stop here)

Just for completeness, host 200.100.206.99 is in subnet 200.100.206.96. You often see me refer to the host number as just one value; here it is 99. By this I mean the value in the hosts part of the subnet address. Of course the full host address is 200.100.206.99 when applied to a host on your network.

Can you see how simple the process is? You must be careful to tick the right boxes in the Subnetting Cheat Chart to start with, or your subnetting results will be entirely wrong.

Example

What is the broadcast address for the subnet host 190.200.200.167/28 is in?

This question never actually matters when you use the Subnetting Cheat Chart because we simply follow the same process and the correct answer will be revealed.

We can see that we have to convert the /28 address into a subnet mask. The subnet mask for /24 is 255.255.255.0, and we need to add 4 to 24 to get 28. We have stolen 4 bits for subnetting, so you need to tick down four boxes in the upper Subnets column to get to 240. Our subnet mask is 255.255.255.240.

Tick 128, 192, 224, and then 240.

1. How many subnets?

$2^4 = 16$

You should know the drill now. Tick down four boxes in the Powers of 2 Subnets column.

	Bits	128	64	32	16	8	4	2	1
Subnets		✓	✓	✓	✓				
128	✓								
192	✓								
224	✓								
240	✓								
248									
252									
254									
255									
Powers of Two	Subnets	Hosts Minus 2							
2	✓	✓							
4	✓	✓							
8	✓	✓							
16	✓	✓							
32									
64									
128									
256									
512									
1024									
2048									
4096									
8192									
16384									

2. How many hosts per subnet?

We have 4 bits left for the hosts.

$2^4 - 2 = 14$

So we have 16 subnets, each containing 14 hosts.

3. What are the valid subnets?

256 - 240 = 16, or tick four along the very top.

So our subnets are going up in increments of 16 (starting at 0).

0, 16, 32, 48, 64, 80, up to 240

4. What are the valid hosts per subnet / broadcast address?

Subnet	0	16	32	48	64	80	96	112	128	144	160	176	192	208	224	240
First host	1	17	33	49	65	81	97	113	129	145	161	177	193	209	225	241
Last host	14	30	46	62	78	94	110	126	142	158	174	190	206	222	238	254
Broadcast	15	31	47	63	79	95	111	127	143	159	175	191	207	223	239	255

Our subnets are:

190.200.200.0, hosts 1-14 (15 is the broadcast)
190.200.200.16, hosts 17-30 (31 is the broadcast)
Multiply 16 by 10 next to save time (jump strategy).
190.200.200.160, hosts 161-174 ← **175 is the broadcast.**
190.200.200.176

Following the same process, we can see that the broadcast address for host 190.200.200.167 is 192.200.200.175 and the subnet address is 190.200.200.160.

Example

Which subnet is host 200.100.55.86/29 in?

By now you should be familiar with ticking down in the Subnetting Cheat Chart. Make sure you continue to use it for the examples. We need to work out how many to add to /24 to get to /29; the answer is 5 of course, so tick down five in the Subnets column to get your mask of 255.255.255.248.

	Bits	128	64	32	16	8	4	2	1
Subnets		✓	✓	✓	✓	✓			
128	✓								
192	✓								
224	✓								
240	✓								
248	✓								
252									
254									
255									
Powers of Two	Subnets	Hosts Minus 2							
2	✓	✓							
4	✓	✓							
8	✓	✓							
16	✓								
32	✓								

1. How many subnets?

$2^5 = 32$

2. How many hosts per subnet?

$2^3 - 2 = 6$

3. What are the valid subnets?

256 - 248 = 8, or tick five across the top row.

So we will go up in increments of 8. We don't have the space to count up all the way to 248 in multiples of 8. In the exam you won't have time to do it either, so you can skip to the number closest to the subnet you are being asked, such as 40, 80, 120, etc. Just make sure the number is divisible by 8.

4. What are the valid hosts per subnet / broadcast address?

Subnet	0	8	16	24	etc.	80	88	etc.	248
First host	1	9	17	25	etc.	81	89	etc.	249
Last host	6	14	22	30	etc.	86	94	etc.	254
Broadcast	7	15	23	31	etc.	87	95	etc.	255

The subnets are:

200.100.55.0
200.100.55.8 ← **multiply 8 by 10 (jump strategy)**
200.100.55.80, hosts 81-86 ← **host 86 here**
200.100.55.88

Host 200.100.55.86 is in subnet 200.100.55.80.

Example

Which subnet is host 210.25.200.165/30 in?

We use a 30-bit subnet mask for subnets that need only two hosts. A point-to-point connection is ideal for this.

You should now write out your own Subnetting Cheat Chart to get into the habit you will need for the exam. There is a blank Subnetting Cheat Chart at the end of Part 2 for you to use; you do need to write it out by hand in IT exams or interviews though.

We need to get to /30 from the default /24 mask, so tick down six in the top Subnets column, which gives you a mask of 255.255.255.252.

1. How many subnets?

$2^6 = 64$

2. How many hosts per subnet?

$2^2 - 2 = 2$

3. What are the valid subnets?

256 - 252 = 4, or tick six places across the top row.

0, 4, 8, 12, 16, etc., up to 252

FOR THE EXAM: Be careful not to go up to 8 and then double it—i.e., 4, 8, 16. This is a very common mistake to make when a person is under pressure.

---

4. What are the valid hosts per subnet / broadcast address?

Subnet	0	4	8	12	16	etc.	160	164	etc.	252
First host	1	5	9	13	17	etc.	161	165	etc.	253
Last host	2	6	10	14	18	etc.	162	166	etc.	254
Broadcast	3	7	11	15	19	etc.	163	167	etc.	255

Be careful not to spend an age counting up in multiples of 4 in the exam. I always look at the host number (165 in this example) and multiply the subnet 4 or 8 by 10. If we need to get to host 165, I would multiply 16 by 10, which gives the subnet 160 (which is still a multiple of 4).

Subnet 210.25.200.0
Subnet 210.25.200.4
Subnet 210.25.200.8
Subnet 210.25.200.16 ← **jump here (16 × 10 = 160)**
Subnet 210.25.200.160, hosts 161-162 (broadcast 163)
Subnet 210.25.200.164, hosts 165-166 (broadcast 167) ← **host 165 here**
Subnet 210.25.200.168

Host 210.25.200.165 is in subnet 210.25.200.164.

CLASS B SUBNETTING

The principles for subnetting Class B addresses are exactly the same as those for Class C. You just need to remember that the default subnet mask for Class B addresses is 255.255.0.0, so the subnetting will take place from the third octet onward.

Here are all the possible Class B subnets:

# Bits	Subnet Mask	CIDR	# Subnets	# Hosts
0	255.255.0.0	/16	1 (network)	65534
1	255.255.128.0	/17	2	32766
2	255.255.192.0	/18	4	16382
3	255.255.224.0	/19	8	8190
4	255.255.240.0	/20	16	4094
5	255.255.248.0	/21	32	2046
6	255.255.252.0	/22	64	1022
7	255.255.254.0	/23	128	510
8	255.255.255.0	/24	256	254
9	255.255.255.128	/25	512	126
10	255.255.255.192	/26	1024	62
11	255.255.255.224	/27	2048	30
12	255.255.255.240	/28	4096	14
13	255.255.255.248	/29	8192	6
14	255.255.255.252	/30	16384	2

Table 2.2—All possible Class B subnets

Example

255.255.128.0 or /17

We need to get the hard one out of the way first. The usual rules do not apply, so read through and then come back to this later.

We can use the 0 subnet in the third octet as long as we have some hosts bits turned on in the fourth octet. Unfortunately, you have to think in binary to understand this example.

The /17 part indicates that we have added 1 bit to the default /16 mask to use it for subnetting. Tick one down the upper Subnets column, which gives us the mask 255.255.128.0. We don't write the chart out twice to generate 16 host bits. I put '+8' on the top right to remind you that this is the third octet.

	Bits	128	64	32	16	8	4	2	1 +8
Subnets		✓							
128	✓								
192									
224									
240									
248									
252									
254									
255									
Powers of Two	Subnets	Hosts Minus 2							
2	✓	✓							
4		✓							
8		✓							
16		✓							
32		✓							
64		✓							
128		✓							
256		✓							
512		✓							
1024		✓							
2048		✓							
4096		✓							
8192		✓							
16384		✓							
32768		✓							
65536									

1. How many subnets?

Our increment is 128. This means we can have 0 and 128, so we get two subnets ($2^1 = 2$). You can see this by the one tick we have added to the lower Subnets column (for the 1 bit we have stolen).

2. How many hosts per subnet?

We have 7 bits left in the third octet and 8 in the fourth (hence the '+8' in the Subnetting Cheat Chart), giving us 15 host bits all together.

$2^{15} - 2 = 32,766$

We can't really follow the rest of the subnetting questions for the 128 mask because the /17 mask is the exception. We do know though that we can have 0 in the third octet as long as we have no bits turned on in the fourth octet.

Subnet	0.0	128.0
First host	0.1	128.1
Last host	127.254	255.254
Broadcast	127.255	255.255

So if our host address is 120.100.55.86/17, our subnets will be:

120.100.0.0, hosts 0.1-127.254 (broadcast 127.255) ← **host 120.100.55.86 here**
120.100.128.0, hosts 128.1-255.254 (broadcast 255.255)

Host 120.100.55.86 is in subnet 120.100.0.0.

Above you can see I refer to just the last two octets when quoting the host numbers—for example, hosts 0.1 and 127.254. This notation makes sense to me; other people prefer to write out the entire four octets when quoting the addresses. Use what works for you.

Example

What subnet is host 150.200.155.23/18 in?

The trick is to remember that we are still subnetting in the third octet. The default mask for Class B is 255.255.0.0, which is 16 binary bits. We need to add 2 to 16 to get to our /18 mask, so tick down two in the top Subnets column. Our subnet mask then is 255.255.192.0.

This will leave 6 host bits in the third octet and another 8 in the fourth octet (6 + 8 = 14 host bits). I don't need that '+8' on the right of the chart because I know where I am, so you can remove it anytime if you feel confident.

	Bits	128	64	32	16	8	4	2	1
Subnets		✓	✓						
128	✓								
192	✓								
224									
240									
248									
252									
254									
255									
Powers of Two	Subnets	Hosts Minus 2							
2	✓	✓							
4	✓	✓							
8		✓							
16		✓							
32		✓							
64		✓							
128		✓							
256		✓							
512		✓							
1024		✓							
2048		✓							
4096		✓							
8192		✓							
16384		✓							

1. How many subnets?

$2^2 = 4$ (indicated by ticking down two in the Powers of 2 Subnets column)

2. How many hosts per subnet?

For this question you are going to have to use your imagination to extend the Subnetting Cheat Chart. The bits all represent the octet we are subnetting. If we subnet across two subnets, we will need to remember how many host bits are left.

In this example we have stolen 2 bits from the third octet, which leaves 6 bits in the third octet plus 8 in the fourth octet, giving us 14 bits. Tick down 14 host bits in the hosts column.

$2^{14} - 2 = 16,382$

3. What are the valid subnets?

256 - 192 = 64 (or tick two across the top row)

0, 64, 128, 192

4. What are the valid hosts per subnet / broadcast address?

Subnet	0.0	64.0	128.0	192.0
First host	0.1	64.1	128.1	192.1
Last host	63.254	127.254	191.254	255.254
Broadcast	63.255	127.255	191.255	255.255

The above numbers are the third and fourth octets. You could write out the entire subnet (as below), but this does take a lot longer.

So our subnets are:

150.200.0.0, hosts 0.1 to 63.254 (broadcast 150.200.63.255)
150.200.64.0, hosts 64.1 to 127.254 (broadcast 150.200.127.255)
150.200.128.0, hosts 128.1 to 191.254 (broadcast 150.200.191.255) ← host
150.200.155.23 in here
150.200.192.0, hosts 192.1 to 255.254 (broadcast 150.200.255.255)

Host 155.23 is within host numbers 128.1 to 191.254 in subnet 3.

Host 150.200.155.23 is in subnet 150.200.128.0.

Example

Which subnet is host 160.24.67.200/19 in?

Can you write out your own Subnetting Cheat Chart for this one yourself?

What do we have to add to /16 to get a mask of /19, and how many bits do we tick down and across the top?

1. How many subnets?

$2^3 = 8$

2. How many hosts per subnet?

$2^{13} - 2 = 8190$

3. What are the valid subnets?

256 - 224 = 32 (or tick three across the top)

0, 32, 64, 96, 128, 160, 192, 224

4. What are the valid hosts per subnet / broadcasts?

Subnet	0.0	32.0	64.0	96.0	128.0	160.0	192.0	224.0
First host	0.1	32.1	64.1	96.1	128.1	160.1	192.1	224.1
Last host	31.254	63.254	95.254	127.254	159.254	191.254	223.254	255.254
Broadcast	31.255	63.255	95.255	127.255	159.255	191.255	223.255	255.255

Can you look at the table above and see which subnet host 67.200 is in?

The answer is subnet 160.24.64.0 contains host 160.24.67.200.

What if you were asked what the broadcast address for this subnet is?

Example

Which subnet is host 190.50.100.200/20 in?

Write out a Subnetting Cheat Chart again.

How many do we tick down to get to /20 from the /16 default mask? Tick the same number across the top to get the increment.

1. How many subnets?

$2^4 = 16$

2. How many hosts per subnet?

$2^{12} - 2 = 4094$

3. What are the valid subnets?

$256 - 240 = 16$

0, 16, 32, 48, 64, and so on up to 240. We can't fit them all in below.

4. What are the valid hosts per subnet / broadcasts?

Subnet	0.0	16.0	32.0	48.0	64.0	80.0	96.0	112.0	etc.	240.0
First host	0.1	16.1	32.1	48.1	64.1	80.1	96.1	112.1		240.1
Last host	15.254	31.254	47.254	63.254	79.254	95.254	111.254	127.254		255.254
Broadcast	15.255	31.255	47.255	63.255	79.255	95.255	111.255	127.255		255.255

We are looking for host 100.200, which is in the 96.0 subnet.

Host 190.50.100.200 is in the 190.50.96.0 subnet.

Example

Which subnet is host 180.22.56.65/21 in?

Follow the procedure for the previous examples to determine the correct mask for the /21 subnet.

1. How many subnets?

$2^5 = 32$

2. How many hosts per subnet?

$2^{11} - 2 = 2046$

3. What are the valid subnets?

256 - 248 = 8

0, 8, 16, 24, 32, 40,..., 248, or in full:

180.22.0.0
180.22.8.0
180.22.16.0, etc.

4. What are the valid hosts per subnet / broadcasts?

Subnet	0.0	8.0	16.0	24.0	32.0	40.0	48.0	56.0	etc.
First host	0.1	8.1	16.1	24.1	32.1	40.1	48.1	56.1	
Last host	7.254	15.254	23.254	31.254	39.254	47.254	55.254	63.254	
Broadcast	7.255	15.255	23.255	31.255	39.255	47.255	55.255	63.255	

Subnet	192.0	200.0	208.0	216.0	224.0	232.0	240.0	248.0
First host	192.1	200.1	208.1	216.1	224.1	232.1	240.1	248.1
Last host	199.254	207.254	215.254	223.254	231.254	239.254	247.254	255.254
Broadcast	199.255	207.255	215.255	223.255	231.255	239.255	247.255	255.255

We can't fit all of the available subnets in, and in the exam, you will just want to find the answer as quickly as possible. Anything before or after the relevant subnet is of no concern to you (apart from working out the correct subnet).

The correct subnet for the host 180.22.56.65 is 180.22.56.0.

Are you starting to understand how it all works now? You may have understood this in the first go, or it may take what seems like an age for it to sink in. How long it takes has nothing to do with how clever you are. Previous IT experience will help, but a lot of it will be down to when you last studied and whether the left or right side of your brain is the dominant one.

Don't force it in. Just follow the process over and over and you will get it, guaranteed.

One more thing: Don't be surprised if it clicks into place all of a sudden and then goes away again. This is very common and a sign that the information is passing from short- to long-term memory. It will come back again.

Example

Which subnet is host 180.100.60.85/23 in?

Use the Subnetting Cheat Chart to determine the subnet mask and subnet increment, etc.

1. How many subnets?

$2^7 = 128$

2. How many hosts per subnet?

$2^9 - 2 = 510$

3. What are the valid subnets?

$256 - 254 = 2$

0, 2, 4, 6, 8, etc., 250, 252, 254

4. What are the valid hosts per subnet / broadcasts?

Subnet	0.0	2.0	4.0	6.0	etc.	60.0	etc.	254.0
First host	0.1	2.1	4.1	6.1		60.1		254.1
Last host	1.254	3.254	5.254	7.254		61.254		255.254
Broadcast	1.255	3.255	5.255	7.255		61.255		255.255

You could jump from 6.0 to 60.0, which would hit the 60.85 host straightaway as the next subnet would be 62.0. Host 180.100.60.85 is in subnet 180.100.60.0.

Example

Which subnet is host 130.100.200.121/24 in?

No, your eyes are not deceiving you. Don't look at this subnet and think Class C; it is in this instance 8 bits of subnetting being used for a Class B address. Do not ponder too long over it; just follow the usual procedure.

Use the Subnetting Cheat Chart.

1. How many subnets?

$2^8 = 256$

2. How many hosts per subnet?

$2^8 - 2 = 254$

3. What are the valid subnets?

256 - 255 = 1 (or tick across eight places)

0, 1, 2, 3, 4, 5, and so on up to 255

4. What are the valid hosts per subnet / broadcasts?

Subnet	0.0	1.0	2.0	3.0	etc.	254.0	255.0
First host	0.1	1.1	2.1	3.1		254.1	255.1
Last host	0.254	1.254	2.254	3.254		254.254	255.254
Broadcast	0.255	1.255	2.255	3.255		254.255	255.255

So if you just keep counting up in increments of 1, you will reach subnet 200.0. Host 130.100.200.121 is therefore in subnet 130.100.200.0.

Example

Which subnet is host 191.20.56.65 255.255.255.128 in?

This one is a bit easier because the (/25) subnet is written out in longhand for you already. Nine bits have been taken for use in subnetting. This is another tricky example which does not fit neatly into the usual formula we use. We can take 128 from 256 for the subnet increment but also count up in increments of 1 in the third octet!

We are also allowed to have a 0 in the third octet if we have a bit turned on in the fourth octet. For each value such as subnet 10 you get 10.0 and then 10.128. If you remember that, you will be fine. In the Subnetting Cheat Chart you might want to put a '+8' in the top LEFT box to remind you that we have spilled over into octet 4 from octet 3.

1. How many subnets?

$2^9 = 512$

2. How many hosts per subnets?

$2^7 - 2 = 126$

3. What are the valid subnets?

256 - 128 = 128 (but we also count in increments of 1 in the third octet)

0, 1, 2, 3, 4, 5, etc., 255

Because we are subnetting in the fourth octet, we can actually use the 0 subnet in the third octet. This is possible because if we have a bit turned on in the fourth octet, we do not have all the host bits off. We can also use 255 in the last octet.

If this doesn't make much sense at the moment, there is no need for concern. It is very doubtful you will come across this in exams or interviews, but then again it is a useful subnet for use in the real world, so you never know! You can write this out in binary later when you have time.

4. What are the valid hosts per subnet / broadcasts?

Subnet	0.0	0.128	1.0	1.128	2.0	2.128	etc.	255.0	255.128
First host	0.1	0.129	1.1	1.129	2.1	2.129		255.1	255.129
Last host	0.126	0.254	1.126	1.254	2.126	2.254		255.126	255.254
Broadcast	0.127	0.255	1.127	1.255	2.127	2.255		255.127	255.255

Host 191.20.56.65 is in subnet 191.20.56.0. There isn't room to fill in every subnet value above, but you can see that the subnets would go up as follows:

191.20.55.0
191.20.55.128
191.20.56.0 ← **Host 191.20.56.65 is in here.**
191.20.56.128
191.20.57.0, etc.

Example

Which subnet is host 180.100.1.220/27 in?

We have skipped the /26 subnet. The principles are exactly the same. Remember to use the Subnetting Cheat Chart to save time and to make sure that your answer is correct. You are hitting the fourth octet in this example, so you would just tick down three places (because you can't fit in the 8 bits in the third octet in the chart).

Just bear in mind here that we have a Class B address with the default mask of /16, which means we are using 11 bits for subnetting, leaving 5 bits for hosts per subnet.

	Bits	128	64	32	16	8	4	2	1
Subnets		✓	✓	✓					
128	✓								
192	✓								
224	✓								
240									
248									
252									
254									
255									
Powers of Two	Subnets	Hosts Minus 2							
2	✓	✓							
4	✓	✓							
8	✓	✓							
16	✓	✓							
32	✓	✓							
64	✓								
128	✓								
256	✓								
512	✓								
1024	✓								
2048	✓								
4096									
8192									
16384									

1. How many subnets?

$2^{11} = 2048$

2. How many hosts per subnet?

$2^5 - 2 = 30$

3. What are the valid subnets?

256 - 224 = 32

0.0, 0.32, 0.64, 0.96, etc., 255.32, 255.64, etc., 255.192, 255.224

4. What are the valid hosts per subnet / broadcasts?

As before, if all of this doesn't make much sense, then let me assure you that this is normal. This is all based on binary mathematics, but because we are using the fast decimal method, it will just never look right. Keep on working through the examples and they will eventually make perfect sense—honest!

We can manipulate the third octet due to the fact that we can have bits on and off in the fourth octet. There are too many subnets to write out, but we can write out some.

Subnet	0.0	0.32	0.64	0.96	0.128	0.160	0.192	0.224
First host	0.1	0.33	0.65	0.97	0.129	0.161	0.193	0.225
Last host	0.30	0.62	0.94	0.126	0.158	0.190	0.222	0.254
Broadcast	0.31	0.63	0.95	0.127	0.159	0.191	0.223	0.255

The above example works because as long as we can have bits turned on in the fourth octet, we can have all the bits off in the third octet.

Next, we can turn bits on in the third octet.

Subnet	1.0	1.32	1.64	1.96	1.128	1.192	1.224
First host	1.1	1.33	1.65	1.97	1.129	1.193	1.225
Last host	1.30	1.62	1.94	1.126	1.190	1.222	1.254
Broadcast	1.31	1.63	1.95	1.127	1.191	1.223	1.255

We can continue subnetting until we get to number 255 in the third octet. We can go all the way up to subnet 255.224.

1.1.1.1.1.1.1.1|1.1.1.1.1.1.1.1|1.1.1.1.1.1.1.1|1.1.0.1.1.1.1.1
Subnet --| Host bits

All the subnet bits we can turn on are on. We can't have 1.1.1 for the first 3 subnet bits since this is the number 224, which is our subnet. When we turn on the last 5 bits (the host bits), this is a broadcast in the 255.192 subnet.

Subnet	255.0	255.32	255.64	255.96	255.128	255.160	255.192	255.224
First host	255.1	255.33	255.65	255.97	255.129	255.161	255.193	255.225
Last host	255.30	255.62	255.94	255.126	255.158	255.190	255.222	255.254
Broadcast	255.31	255.63	255.95	255.127	255.159	255.191	255.223	255.255

Host 180.100.1.220 is in subnet 180.100.1.192.

If you want a superfast exam cheat method, then just ignore the fact we are using a Class B address. Just focus on the last octet instead and count up in increments of 32, fixing the first three octets as follows:

180.100.1.0
180.100.1.32
180.100.1.64, etc.

Example

Which subnet is host 150.60.200.107/28 in?

Use the Subnetting Cheat Chart again. The mask will be 255.255.255.240. The chart will have to be used to represent the last octet. Taking the 12 masked bits we have stolen, we have to presume we have ticked across the first 8 bits for the third octet and have spilled over to the fourth octet and tick the remaining 4 bits.

	Bits	128	64	32	16	8	4	2	1
Subnets		✓	✓	✓	✓				
128	✓								
192	✓								
224	✓								
240	✓								
248									
252									
254									
255									
Powers of Two	Subnets	Hosts Minus 2							
2	✓	✓							
4	✓	✓							
8	✓	✓							
16	✓	✓							
32	✓								
64	✓								
128	✓								
256	✓								
512	✓								
1024	✓								
2048	✓								
4096	✓								

1. How many subnets?

$2^{12} = 4096$

2. How many hosts per subnet?

$2^4 - 2 = 14$

3. What are the valid subnets?

256 - 240 = 16

0, 16, 32, 48, 64, 80, 96, etc., 208, 224, 240

4. What are the valid hosts per subnet / broadcasts?

The same rules apply as in the previous example. We can have all the bits off in the third octet as long as we have subnet bits on in the fourth octet.

Here are the first subnets:

Subnet	0.0	0.16	0.32	0.48	0.64	0.96	etc.	0.240
First host	0.1	0.17	0.33	0.49	0.65	0.97		0.241
Last host	0.14	0.30	0.46	0.62	0.94	0.111		0.254
Broadcast	0.15	0.31	0.47	0.63	0.95	0.112		0.255

Here are more subnets:

Subnet	1.0	1.16	1.32	1.48	1.64	1.80	1.96	1.112
First host	1.1	1.17	1.33	1.49	1.65	1.81	1.97	1.113
Last host	1.14	1.30	1.46	1.62	1.78	1.94	1.110	1.126
Broadcast	1.15	1.31	1.47	1.63	1.79	1.95	1.111	1.127

Here are some more subnets:

Subnet	200.48	200.64	200.80	200.96	200.112	200.128	200.144	200.160
First host	200.49	200.65	200.81	200.97	200.113	200.129	200.145	200.161
Last host	200.62	200.78	200.94	200.110	200.126	200.142	200.158	200.174
Broadcast	200.63	200.79	200.95	200.111	200.127	200.143	200.159	200.175

Here are the last subnets.

Subnet	255.0	255.16	255.32	255.48	255.64	etc.	255.223	255.240
First host	255.1	255.17	255.33	255.49	255.65		255.224	255.241
Last host	255.14	255.30	255.46	255.62	255.78		255.238	255.254
Broadcast	255.15	255.31	255.47	255.63	255.79		255.239	255.255

Host 150.60.200.107 is in subnet 150.60.200.96. The full details for the subnet are:

Subnet 150.60.200.96, hosts 97-110, broadcast 111

SUBNETTING IN YOUR HEAD

You can actually do subnetting without writing anything down. It does take a bit of practice, but you will be able to read the question and know the right answer without even seeing the available answers.

Example

What subnet is 192.168.10.90 255.255.255.192 in?

Can you take 192 away from 256 in your head?

You should come to 64. If you start with the first subnet as 0, then you have 64, the next is 128, and the last is 192. You can see the host number is 90, which is less than 128 and more than 64, so we know it is in the .64 subnet somewhere.

Host 192.168.10.90 is in subnet 192.168.10.64.

Example

What subnet is 172.16.20.112 255.255.255.224 in?

Take 224 away from 256, which gives you 32. We can keep adding 32 until we come to the subnet containing 112 as an address: not 32, not 64, could be in 96, 96 plus 32 is 128—bingo! It is in the 172.16.20.96 subnet.

As I mentioned earlier, in the exam, just focus on the octet you are subnetting in. Starting off with 172.16.0.0 is fine when you are in an office designing subnets, but in the exam, start at the octet the last part of the subnet mask is in.

In any exam or interview question, any of the subnets taken away from 256 will result in increments of 2, 4, 8, 16, 32, 64, or 128. As you do more examples, you will remember what taken away from 256 equals what. You will instantly know that 256 - 224 = 32 or that 256 - 240 = 16. Once you have the result of that simple mental calculation, you have everything you need. Simple, isn't it?

Subnetting is like riding a bicycle: the more you practice, the more natural it becomes. You will get to a point where you can look at an IP address and subnet mask and instantly know which subnet it belongs to.

CLASS A SUBNETTING

The principles are exactly the same for Class A subnetting as they are for Classes B and C. We just have more host bits available. We are going to keep this section fairly short since by now you have everything you need to answer any subnetting question.

Bits	Subnet Mask	CIDR	Subnets	Hosts
0	255.0.0.0	/8	1	16777216
1	255.128.0.0	/9	2	8388606
2	255.192.0.0	/10	4	4194302
3	255.224.0.0	/11	8	2097150
4	255.240.0.0	/12	16	1048574
5	255.248.0.0	/13	302	524286
6	255.252.0.0	/14	64	262142
7	255.254.0.0	/15	128	131070
8	255.255.0.0	/16	256	65534
9	255.255.128.0	/17	512	32766
10	255.255.192.0	/18	1024	16382
11	255.255.224.0	/19	2048	8190
12	255.255.240.0	/20	4096	4094
13	255.255.248.0	/21	8192	2046
14	255.255.252.0	/22	16384	1022
15	255.255.254.0	/23	32768	510
16	255.255.255.0	/24	65536	254
17	255.255.255.128	/25	131072	126
18	255.255.255.192	/26	262144	62
19	255.255.255.224	/27	524288	30
20	255.255.255.240	/28	1048576	14
21	255.255.255.248	/29	2097152	6
22	255.255.255.252	/30	4194304	2

Table 2.3—Class A subnets

Example

Which subnet is 10.100.100.93/10 in?

Remember that the default subnet mask for a Class A address is 255.0.0.0 (or /8), so we have 24 bits available for hosts or for subnetting. We will need to add 2 host bits to the Subnetting Cheat Chart to get to the /10 value and to calculate the subnet and hosts per subnet.

	Bits	128	64	32	16	8	4	2	1
Subnets		✓	✓						
128	✓								
192	✓								
224									
240									
248									
252									
254									
255									
Powers of Two	Subnets	Hosts Minus 2							
2	✓	✓							
4	✓	✓							
8		✓							
16		✓							
32		✓							
64		✓							
128		✓							
256		✓							
512		✓							
1024		✓							
2048		✓							
4096		✓							
8192		✓							
16384		✓							
32768		✓							
65536		✓							
131072		✓							
262144		✓							
524288		✓							
1048576		✓							
2097152		✓							
4194304		✓							

1. How many subnets?

$2^2 = 4$

2. How many hosts per subnets?

$2^{22} - 2 = 4,194,302$

3. What are the valid subnets?

$256 - 192 = 64$

0, 64, 128, 192, or if you want to write out all the octets:

10.0.0.0, 10.64.0.0, 10.128.0.0, 10.192.0.0

4. What are the valid hosts per subnet / broadcasts?

Subnet	10.0.0.0	10.64.0.0	10.128.0.0	10.192.0.0
First host	10.0.0.1	10.64.0.1	10.128.0.1	10.192.1
Last host	10.63.255.254	10.127.255.254	10.191.255.254	10.255.255.254
Broadcast	10.63.255.255	10.127.255.255	10.191.255.255	10.255.255.255

Host 10.100.100.93 is in subnet 10.64.0.0.

Note: Exams such as CCNA and CompTIA Network+ are usually pretty fair, so I would be surprised if Cisco gave you a subnetting question that would clearly take considerable time to work out (such as working out powers of two to 22 places as above). It is always better to train using the hard questions though, and then the exam questions will appear easy to you.

Example

Which subnet is host 10.210.204.70/12 in?

How many bits are we using for subnetting here? Are we subnetting in the first, second, or third octet?

1. How many subnets?

$2^4 = 16$

2. How many hosts per subnet?

$2^{20} - 2 = 1,048,574$

3. What are the valid subnets?

256 - 240 = 16 (or tick across the subnets four places)

10.0.0.0
10.16.0.0
10.32.0.0 ← **jump here (6 × 32 = 192)**
10.192.0.0
10.208.0.0 ← **host 10.210.204.70 in here**
10.224.0.0
10.240.0.0

4. What are the valid hosts per subnet / broadcasts?

Subnet	10.0.0.0	10.16.0.0	10.32.0.0	etc.	10.208.0.0	10.224.0.0
First host	10.0.0.1	10.16.0.1	10.32.0.1		10.208.0.1	10.224.0.1
Last host	10.15.255.254	10.31.255.254	10.47.255.254		10.223.255.254	10.255.255.254
Broadcast	10.15.255.255	10.31.255.255	10.47.255.255		10.223.255.255	10.255.255.255

Host 10.210.204.70 is in subnet 10.208.0.0.

Example

Which subnet is host 10.200.100.107/20 in?

Remember that we will have to use the chart for spillover bits from the third octet. You would have ticked 8 bits for the subnets in the second octet, leaving 4 bits to tick in the chart for the third octet.

1. How many subnets?

$2^{12} = 4096$

2. How many hosts per subnet?

$2^{12} - 2 = 4094$

3. What are the valid subnets?

256 - 240 = 16 (or tick across four places)

I have written the subnets out in full this time, but I could have just as easily written 0.0, 16.0, 32.0, etc.

10.0.0.0
10.0.16.0
10.0.32.0
10.0.48.0, etc.
10.1.0.0
10.1.16.0, etc.
10.1.240.0
10.2.0.0
10.2.16.0, etc., up to
10.255.240.0

4. What are the valid hosts per subnet / broadcasts?

We can use 0 in the third octet as before as long as we turn on a subnet bit in the second octet. We could start with 0 in the second octet if we wish as long as we turn on a bit in the third octet.

There are far too many to write out here, so we will have to skip most of the subnets.

Subnet	10.0.0.0	10.0.16.0	10.0.32.0	etc.	10.0.224.0	10.0.240.0
First host	10.0.0.1	10.0.16.1	10.0.32.1		10.0.224.1	10.0.240.1
Last host	10.0.15.254	10.0.31.254	10.0.47.254		10.0.239.254	10.0.255.254
Broadcast	10.0.15.255	10.0.31.255	10.0.47.255		10.0.239.255	10.0.255.255

Some more subnets:

Subnet	10.1.0.0	10.1.16.0	10.1.32.0	etc.	10.1.224.0	10.1.240.0
First host	10.1.0.1	10.1.16.1	10.1.32.1		10.1.224.1	10.1.240.1
Last host	10.1.15.254	10.1.31.254	10.1.47.254		10.1.239.254	10.1.255.254
Broadcast	10.1.15.255	10.1.31.255	10.1.47.255		10.1.239.255	10.1.255.255

Some more subnets:

Subnet	10.200.48.0	10.200.64.0	10.200.80.0	10.200.96.0	10.200.112.0
First host	10.200.48.1	10.200.64.1	10.200.80.1	10.200.96.1	10.200.112.1
Last host	10.200.63.254	10.200.79.254	10.200.95.254	10.200.111.254	10.200.127.254
Broadcast	10.200.63.255	10.200.79.255	10.200.95.255	10.200.111.255	10.200.127.255

Host 10.200.100.107 is in subnet 10.200.96.0.

Subnet 10.200.96.0, hosts 10.200.96.1-10.200.111.254 (broadcast 10.200.111.255)

Remember that the exam cheat method lets you fix parts of the network and work only on the part the last subnet value is in. This would let us do this instead:

10.200.0.0
10.200.16.0
10.200.32.0 ← jump here (3 × 32 = 96)
10.200.96.0 ← host 10.200.100.107 in here
10.200.112.0

It can get fairly hard when working out Class A subnets with what are traditionally thought of as Class B or C subnet masks. I would recommend working on these examples over and over until they start to make sense.

Example

Which subnet is host 20.100.55.3/26 in?

1. How many subnets?

$2^{18} = 262,144$

2. How many hosts per subnet?

$2^6 - 2 = 62$

3. What are the valid subnets?

256 - 192 = 64 (or tick across the top Subnets row two places)

20.0.0.0
20.0.0.64
20.0.0.128, etc.
20.0.14.192
20.0.15.0, etc.

4. What are the valid hosts per subnet / broadcasts?

The subnet values need to be added to the second, third, and fourth octets. The last octet must be multiples of 64, and 0 is permitted as long as there are bits turned on in the second and third octets. Below are the starting subnets.

Subnet	20.0.0.0	20.0.0.64	20.0.0.128	20.0.0.192	20.0.1.0
First host	20.0.0.1	20.0.0.65	20.0.0.129	20.0.0.193	20.0.1.1
Last host	20.0.0.62	20.0.0.126	20.0.0.190	20.0.0.254	20.0.1.62
Broadcast	20.0.0.63	20.0.0.127	20.0.0.191	20.0.0.255	20.0.1.63

And more subnets:

Subnet	20.100.54.128	20.100.54.192	20.100.55.0	20.100.55.64	20.100.55.128
First host	20.100.54.129	20.100.54.193	20.100.55.1	20.100.55.65	20.100.55.129
Last host	20.100.54.190	20.100.54.254	20.100.55.62	20.100.55.126	20.100.55.190
Broadcast	20.100.54.191	20.100.54.255	20.100.55.63	20.100.55.127	20.100.55.191

We could continue counting up, but getting to the subnet containing host 20.100.55.3 would take some time. It is to be found in subnet 20.100.55.0.

Subnet 20.100.55.0, hosts 20.100.55.1-20.100.55.62 (broadcast = 20.100.55.63)

A superfast cheat method is to fix the first three octets and count up in octet four in increments of 64, so:

20.100.55.0 ← **Host 20.100.55.3 is in here.**
20.100.55.64
20.100.55.128

You would still need to use the Subnetting Cheat Chart to get the increment, etc., but doing it this way would reduce your subnetting time for this question to under 60 seconds.

SUPERFAST SUBNETTING

I'm sure that by now, your ability to answer common subnetting questions has improved dramatically.

I've really been drilling you hard, but as I mentioned earlier, in the exam and in technical job interviews, time is of the essence. For this reason you need to be able to answer the specific question asked and then move on.

It's not likely you will be asked to provide the subnet, hosts, broadcast, and number of subnets and hosts all in the same question. It's far more likely you will be asked for just one of these pieces of information.

Example

Which subnet is host 192.168.1.244/28 in?

This time just tick for how many stolen bits there are and then count up until you get the correct subnet. The default is /24, so we have stolen 4 bits. Our increment then is 16.

	Bits	128	64	32	16	8	4	2	1
Subnets		✓	✓	✓	✓				
128	✓								
192	✓								
224	✓								
240	✓								
248									
252									
254									
255									
Powers of Two	Subnets	Hosts Minus 2							
2									
4									
8									
16									
32									
64									
128									
256									
512									
1024									
2048									
4096									
8192									
16384									

Start at the zero subnet and count up in increments of 16 until you get to the correct subnet. Jump up in the increment if you are going to be in a high subnet number.

192.168.1.0
192.168.1.16 ← **Jump up to 160 (16 × 10).**
192.168.1.160
192.168.1.176
192.168.1.192
192.168.1.208
192.168.1.224
192.168.1.240 ← **Host 192.168.1.244 is in here.**

Example

Which subnet is host 172.16.27.100/27 in?

I know you can see a Class B address here, but we have stolen so many bits that we are now into the fourth octet. You COULD start counting up your subnets from 172.16.0.0, BUT this would take a long time and you would reach the same answer as when using my shortcut method.

In exams, just look at the last octet the subnetting goes into and stay there. This applies whether it's Class A or Class B. The smart move here is to treat 172.16.27 as fixed and use the increment to find the subnet the number 100 is in.

I've placed a '+8' in the top left corner of the chart to remind you that we have already stolen 8 bits (from the third octet). /27 from the default /16 is 11, and with 8 bits already taken we add another 3. Our subnet increment then is 32.

+8	Bits	128	64	32	16	8	4	2	1
Subnets		✓	✓	✓					
128	✓								
192	✓								
224	✓								
240									
248									
252									
254									
255									
Powers of Two	Subnets	Hosts Minus 2							
2									
4									
8									
16									
32									
64									
128									
256									
512									
1024									
2048									
4096									
8192									
16384									

172.16.27.0
172.16.27.32
172.16.27.64
172.16.27.96 ← **Host 172.16.27.100 is in here.**
172.16.27.128

If they tag on more information to the question, such as what the broadcast is, then use the five-step method we've used so many times. Alternatively, take 1 away from the next subnet to get your broadcast address. The hosts are located between the subnet and the broadcast address.

For our example the host addresses would be 172.16.27.97 to 172.16.27.126 inclusive.

HOW MANY SUBNETS / HOW MANY HOSTS?

The second type of question you will be asked in the exam is to take a standard IP address and subnet mask and subnet it down further to provide X subnets with X hosts per subnet.

Example

Your client has been given address 192.168.1.0/24 and requires four subnets, and each subnet must be able to provide at least 10 hosts.

Use the Subnetting Cheat Chart and tick down the lower Subnets column next to the powers of two until you reach a value that will give you a minimum of four subnets.

	Bits	128	64	32	16	8	4	2	1
Subnets									
128	✓								
192	✓								
224									
240									
248									
252									
254									
255									
Powers of Two	Subnets	Hosts Minus 2							
2	✓	✓							
4	✓	✓							
8		✓							
16		✓							
32		✓							
64		✓							
128									
256									
512									
1024									
2048									
4096									
8192									
16384									

Ticking down two boxes gives you the required four subnets. You can now tick down two boxes in the upper Subnets column to generate the correct subnet of 255.255.255.192 (or /26). You have stolen 2 bits from the last octet to generate the subnet mask, leaving 6 for hosts. Tick down six boxes in the hosts column to find out how many hosts per subnet you have.

You have 62 (64 - 2) hosts per subnet, which more than meets the requirement of the client.

Example

You have address 200.100.20.0/24, and the client wants to break this down into at least nine subnets each having at least 10 hosts.

Here you need to generate AT LEAST nine subnets but not waste subnets. Tick down the Powers of 2 Subnets column until you reach the closest possible number to nine without wasting subnets.

	Bits	128	64	32	16	8	4	2	1
Subnets									
128	✓								
192	✓								
224	✓								
240	✓								
248									
252									
254									
255									
Powers of Two	Subnets	Hosts Minus 2							
2	✓	✓							
4	✓	✓							
8	✓	✓							
16	✓	✓							
32									
64									
128									
256									
512									
1024									
2048									
4096									
8192									
16384									

The closest we can get is 16 because 8 is not sufficient. Tick down four places in the upper Subnets column to generate a subnet mask of 255.255.255.240. You have taken 4 bits from the last subnet, leaving 4 for hosts.

16 - 2 gives us 14 hosts per subnet, which is sufficient.

Example

Your client has IP address 130.100.0.0/16 and requires 30 subnets each having at least 1000 hosts. Generate a subnet mask that meets this requirement.

Same deal, but remember that we are taking bits from the third octet.

	Bits	128	64	32	16	8	4	2	1
Subnets									
128	✓								
192	✓								
224	✓								
240	✓								
248	✓								
252									
254									
255									
Powers of Two	Subnets	Hosts Minus 2							
2	✓	✓							
4	✓	✓							
8	✓	✓							
16	✓	✓							
32	✓	✓							
64		✓							
128		✓							
256		✓							
512		✓							
1024		✓							
2048		✓							
4096									
8192									
16384									

We have to tick down five boxes in the Powers of 2 Subnets column to get the value of 32, which is as close as we can get to 30 subnets. This leaves 3 bits in the third octet and 8 bits in the fourth octet for hosts (11 bits).

Five ticks down in the upper Subnets column gives us a subnet of 255.255.248.0.

Tick down 11 places in the hosts column, which gives us 2046 hosts per subnet.

Easy-peasy.

WILDCARD MASKS

Wildcard masks do belong under the umbrella of IP subnetting. Wildcard masks are of particular relevance to network engineers who configure access lists on routers or firewalls or implement OSPF routing on networks. If neither of these applies to you, then please feel free to skip this section.

All the practical examples here pertain to configurations on Cisco routers. If you are working with a different vendor, then the command line and syntax will be different. Cisco offers its network simulation tool Packet Tracer as a free download. Please check out our *101 Labs – CompTIA Network+* or *101 Labs – Cisco CCNA* if you want to see more examples of how to use wildcard masks.

The wildcard mask can be confusing to anybody new to access lists. Just remember that the router reads in binary instead of decimal. The wildcard mask is there to tell the access list which parts of the address to look at. A 1 in binary means that part of the address can be ignored, and a 0 means it must match.

Example

If I want to match all traffic from 172.16.2.x, then I will add the wildcard mask 0.0.0.255, or in binary:

10101100.00010000.00000010.00000000 = 172.16.2.0
00000000.00000000.00000000.11111111 = 0.0.0.255
Match   Match   Match   Ignore

In action this would mean any host from the network starting with 172.16.2.x would match the access list. 172.16.3.x would not match the access list. Example:

Here we have an access list permitting any traffic from the 10.x.x.x network:

```
access-list 9 permit 10.0.0.0 0.255.255.255
```

There is an implicit 'deny all' at the end of Cisco access lists. When you apply this to an interface, the only permitted network will be 10.x.x.x.

```
access-list 9 permit 10.0.0.0 0.255.255.255
(access-list 9 deny 0.0.0.0 255.255.255.255)  ← This is present
```
but you won't see it. It is the 'deny any' command.

Example

```
access-list 12 permit 172.16.2.0 0.0.0.255  ← 172.16.2.x
```
allowed
```
access-list 12 permit 192.168.1.0 0.0.0.255  ← 192.168.1.x
```
allowed
```
access-list 12 permit 10.4.0.0 0.0.255.255  ← 10.4.x.x allowed
```

This access list permits three networks and denies traffic from any other network.

Example

```
access-list 15 deny 172.16.0.0 0.0.255.255
access-list 15 deny 192.168.2.1  ← You can specify a host address.
access-list 15 permit any
```

If you want to deny a few networks, subnets, or hosts and permit the rest, use the logic shown above. We are denying anything from the 172.16.x.x network, but we can also specify a single host without using a wildcard mask. Just enter the host number and the router will automatically add 0.0.0.0 to it.

Lastly, we have added 'permit any' to the end of the list. This is to prevent the implicit 'deny any' from denying any other traffic. If you forget this line, all traffic will be denied.

You can break wildcard masks down from the default subnet boundaries just as you can use VLSM to change the default subnet mask for an IP address.

Example

If you wanted to deny the 192.168.100.96 255.255.255.224 subnet, you would use the following wildcard mask:

0.0.0.31

It will make more sense if we write this out in binary:

11111111 11111111 11111111 11100000 = 255.255.255.224
00000000 00000000 00000000 00011111 = 0.0.0.31

So the access list matches the first 27 bits, and the last 5 can be any. The simplest way to look at this is to swap each on bit with an off bit when you are writing out the wildcard mask.

Example

10.1.64.0 255.255.192.0

If you wanted to permit or deny this subnet, you would need to create a specific wildcard mask to match it. The wildcard mask needs to be the reverse of the subnet mask to permit or deny this subnet.

11111111 11111111 11000000 00000000 = 255.255.192.0
00000000 00000000 00111111 11111111 = 0.0.63.255

So long as you get 255 when you add the two columns together, you know the wildcard mask is correct. This is shown in the example above.

Subnet mask	255	255	192	0
Wildcard mask	0	0	63	255
Equals	255	255	255	255

Example

What wildcard mask would deny the subnet 172.16.32.0 255.255.240.0?

Subnet mask	255	255	240	0
Wildcard mask	0	0	15	255
Equals	255	255	255	255

The access list would read 'permit/deny 172.16.32.0 0.0.15.255'.

Wildcard masks are commonly used with OSPF to advertise specific subnets.

> **FOR THE EXAM:** It would be time well spent to practice your wildcard masks for various subnets, such as 192, 224, 240, etc.

IP Version 6

Despite the existence of subnetting and private IP addresses there is still a need for a new IP addressing system to cater for future demands. IPv4 will not cater for the near future, when every household (and almost every other) device will require its own IP address. IP version 6 is already available and has been implemented by many organizations.

> **FOR THE EXAM:** You may be asked a simple question or be expected to recognize an IPv6 address in your networking exam.

The improvements made over IPv4 in IPv6 are increased addresses, reduced routing table size, and improved security.

HEX NUMBERING

It may well be worthwhile to have a short memory jogger on hex numbering.

You know that decimal numbers consist of 10 digits ranging from 0 to 9. Binary consists of two digits ranging from 0 to 1. Hex numbering ranges from 0 to F and has 16 digits. These addresses are also referred to as base 10, base 2, and base 16, respectively.

You can see that each numbering system starts with a zero, so:

Decimal – 0, 1, 2, 3, 4, 5, 6, 7, 8, 9
Binary – 0, 1
Hex – 0, 1, 2, 3, 4, 5, 6, 7, 8, 9, A, B, C, D, E, F

When you write these addresses, you may not realize it but you are using columns from right to left; the rightmost is the 1 column, and the next column is the base number times the preceding column, so:

Numbering base	N to 3rd power	N to 2nd power	N to 1st power	N
10 – Decimal	1000	100	10	1
2 – Binary	8	4	2	1
16 – Hex	4096	256	16	1

Table 2.4—Powers in decimal, binary, and hexadecimal systems

You can see that each successive column from the right increases in value. For decimal numbering it is 10 multiplied by 1. For binary it is 1 and then 1 multiplied by the numbering system of 2 and of course for 16 the multiples are 16. If you compare the three numbering systems up to the last hex digit, you can begin to see why hex is the preferred format for IPv6 addressing.

Decimal	Binary	Hex
0	0000	0
1	0001	1
2	0010	2
3	0011	3
4	0100	4
5	0101	5
6	0110	6
7	0111	7
8	1000	8
9	1001	9
10	1010	A
11	1011	B
12	1100	C
13	1101	D
14	1110	E
15	1111	F

Table 2.5—Correspondence between the three numbering systems

In order to provide enough addresses for our needs many years into the future, IPv6 has been designed to provide many trillions of addresses.

In order to do this, the numbering range has been expanded from 32 binary bits to 128 bits. Every 4 bits can be represented as one hex digit (as can be seen from the chart above). Logic then dictates that two hex digits give us 8 bits, which is a single byte, or octet.

An IPv6 address is 128 bits in length, and this is broken down into eight sets of 16 bits each separated by a colon when written in full format. Every 4 hex bits can range from 0000 to FFFF, with F being the highest digit available in hex numbering:

0000	0000	0000	0000	0000	0000	0000	0000
to	to	to	to	to	to	to	to
FFFF	FFFF	FFFF	FFFF	FFFF	FFFF	FFFF	FFFF

IPV6 ADDRESSING

As we already know, IPv6 uses 128-bit addresses. Because the address format is different from the IPv4 address format that we are all accustomed to, it is often confusing at first glance. However, once understood, the logic and structure are very simple. The 128-bit IPv6 addresses use hexadecimal values (i.e., numbers 0 through 9 and letters A through F).

While in IPv4 the subnet mask can be represented in either CIDR notation (e.g., /16 or /32) or dotted-decimal notation (e.g., 255.255.0.0 or 255.255.255.255), IPv6 subnet masks are represented only in CIDR notation due to the length of the IPv6 address.

Global 128-bit IPv6 addresses are divided into the following three sections:

- The provider-assigned prefix
- The site prefix
- The interface or host ID

The provider-assigned prefix, which is also referred to as the global address space, is a 48-bit prefix that is divided into the following three distinct parts:

- The 16-bit reserved IPv6 global prefix
- The 16-bit provider-owned prefix
- The 16-bit provider-assigned prefix

The IPv6 global prefix is used to represent the IPv6 global address space. All IPv6 global internet addresses fall within the 2000::/16 to 3FFF::/16 range. The 16-bit provider-owned IPv6 prefix is assigned to and owned by the provider. The assignment of these prefixes follows the same rules as prefix assignment in IPv4. The provider-owned prefix falls within the 0000::/32 to FFFF::/32 range.

The next 16 bits represent an IPv6 prefix assigned to an organization by the actual provider from within the provider-assigned prefix address space. This prefix falls within the 0000::/48 to FFFF::/48 range. Collectively, these first 48 bits are referred to as the provider-assigned prefix, which is illustrated in Figure 2.1 below:

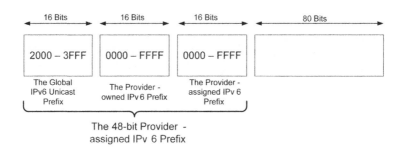

Fig. 2.1—The 48-bit provider-assigned IPv6 prefix

The site prefix is the 16 bits following the 48-bit provider-assigned prefix. The subnet mask length for a site prefix is /64, which includes the 48-bit provider-assigned prefix. This prefix length allows for 264 addresses within each site prefix. Figure 2.2 below illustrates the 16-bit site prefix:

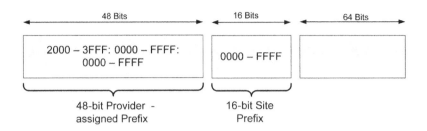

Fig. 2.2—The 16-bit IPv6 site prefix

Following the site prefix, 64 bits are used for interface or host addressing. The interface or host ID portion of an IPv6 address represents the network device or host on the IPv6 subnet. The different ways in which the interface or host address is determined will be described in detail later in this module.

Figure 2.3 below illustrates how IPv6 prefixes are assigned:

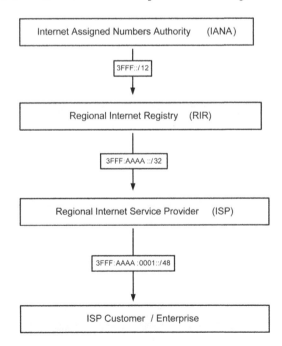

Fig. 2.3—Assigning IPv6 prefixes

Referencing Figure 2.3, once customers have been assigned the /48 prefix by the ISP, they are then free to assign and use whatever site prefixes and host or interface addresses they want within that 48-bit provider-assigned prefix.

The sheer amount of address space available makes it impossible for any single enterprise customer to require more than a single provider-assigned prefix, while still allowing all devices within the enterprise network to be allocated a unique IPv6 global address. NAT, therefore, will never be required for IPv6.

IPV6 ADDRESS REPRESENTATION

The three ways in which IPv6 addresses can be represented are as follows:

- The preferred or complete address representation or form
- Compressed representation
- IPv6 addresses with an embedded IPv4 address

While the preferred form or representation is the one most commonly used for representing the 128-bit IPv6 address in text format, it is also important to be familiar with the other two methods of IPv6 address representation. These methods are described in the following sections.

The Preferred Form

The preferred representation for an IPv6 address is the longest format, also referred to as the complete form of an IPv6 address. This format presents all 32 hexadecimal characters that are used to form an IPv6 address. This is performed by writing the address as a series of eight 16-bit hexadecimal fields separated by a colon (e.g., 3FFF:1234:ABCD:5678:020C:CEFF:FEA 7:F3A0).

Each 16-bit field is represented by four hexadecimal characters, and each character represents 4 bits. Each 16-bit hexadecimal field can have a value between 0x0000 and 0xFFFF, although, as will be described later in this module, different values have been reserved for use in the first 16 bits, so all possible values are not used.

When writing IPv6 addresses, hexadecimal characters are not case sensitive. In other words, 2001:ABCD:0000 and 2001:abcd:0000 are the exact same thing. The complete form for IPv6 address representation is illustrated in Figure 2.4 below:

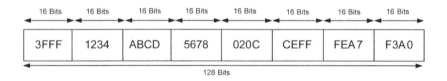

Fig. 2.4—The preferred form for IPv6 address representation

The following IPv6 addresses are examples of valid IPv6 addresses in the preferred form:

- 0000:0000:0000:0000:0000:0000:0000:0001
- 2001:0000:0000:1234:0000:5678:af23:bcd5
- 3FFF:0000:0000:1010:1A2B:5000:0B00:DE0F
- fec0:2004:ab10:00cd:1234:0000:0000:6789
- 0000:0000:0000:0000:0000:0000:0000:0000

Compressed Representation

Compressed representation allows for IPv6 addresses to be compressed in one of two ways. The first method uses a double colon (::) to compress consecutive zero values in a valid IPv6 address for successive 16-bit fields comprised of zeros or for leading zeros in the IPv6 address. When using this method, it is important to remember that the double colon can be used only once in an IPv6 address.

When the compressed format is used, each node and router is responsible for counting the number of bits on either side of the double colon to determine the exact number of zeros it represents. Table 2.6 below shows IPv6 addresses in the preferred form and the compressed representation of those addresses:

Complete IPv6 Address Representation	Compressed IPv6 Address Representation
0000:0000:0000:0000:0000:0000:0000:0001	::0001
2001:0000:0000:1234:0000:5678:af23:bcd5	2001::1234:0000:5678:af23:bcd5
3FFF:0000:0000:1010:1A2B:5000:0B00:DE0F	3FFF::1010:1A2B:5000:0B00:DE0F
FEC0:2004:AB10:00CD:1234:0000:0000:6789	FEC0:2004:AB10:00CD:1234::6789
0000:0000:0000:0000:0000:FFFF:172.16.255.1	::FFFF:172.16.255.1
0000:0000:0000:0000:0000:0000:172.16.255.1	::172.16.255.1
0000:0000:0000:0000:0000:0000:0000:0000	::

Table 2.6—Complete IPv6 addresses in preferred and compressed forms (method 1)

As previously stated, the double colon cannot be used more than once in a single IPv6 address. If, for example, you wanted to represent the complete IPv6 address for 2001:0000:0000:1234:0000:0000:af23:bcd5 in compressed form, you could use the double colon only once even though there are two consecutive strings of zeros within the address.

Therefore, attempting to compress the address to 2001::1234::af23:bcd5 would be considered illegal; however, the same IPv6 address could be compressed to either 2001::1234:0000:0000:af23:bcd5 or 2001:0000:0000:1234::af23:bcd5, depending on preference.

The second method of IPv6 compressed address representation is applicable to each 16-bit field and allows leading zeros to be omitted from the IPv6 address. When using this method, if every bit in the 16-bit field is set to 0, then one zero must be used to represent this field. In this case, not all of the zero values can be omitted.

Table 2.7 below shows IPv6 addresses in the preferred form and how they can be compressed using the second method of IPv6 compressed form representation.

Complete IPv6 Address Representation	Compressed IPv6 Address Representation
0000:0123:0abc:0000:04b0:0678:f000:0001	0:123:abc:0:4b0:678:f000:1
2001:0000:0000:1234:0000:5678:af23:bcd5	2001:0:0:1234:0:5678:af23:bcd5
3FFF:0000:0000:1010:1A2B:5000:0B00:DE0F	3FFF:0:0:1010:1A2B:5000:B00:DE0F
fec0:2004:ab10:00cd:1234:0000:0000:6789	fec0:2004:ab10:cd:1234:0:0:6789
0000:0000:0000:0000:0000:FFFF:172.16.255.1	0:0:0:0:0:FFFF:172.16.255.1
0000:0000:0000:0000:0000:0000:172.16.255.1	0:0:0:0:0:0:172.16.255.1
0000:0000:0000:0000:0000:0000:0000:0000	0:0:0:0:0:0:0:0

Table 2.7—Complete IPv6 addresses in the alternative compressed form (method 2)

While there are two methods of representing the complete IPv6 address in compressed form, it is important to remember that both methods are not mutually exclusive. In other words, these methods can be used at the same time to represent the same IPv6 address.

This is commonly used when the complete IPv6 address contains both consecutive strings of zeros and leading zeros in other fields within the address.

Table 2.8 below shows IPv6 addresses in the complete form that include both consecutive strings of zeros and leading zeros, and how these addresses are represented in the compressed form:

Complete IPv6 Address Representation	Compressed IPv6 Address Representation
0000:0000:0000:0000:1a2b:000c:f123:4567	::1a2b:c:f123:4567
FEC0:0004:AB10:00CD:1234:0000:0000:6789	FEC0:4:AB10:CD:1234::6789
3FFF:0c00:0000:1010:1A2B:0000:0000:DE0F	3FFF:c00:0:1010:1A2B::DE0F
2001:0000:0000:1234:0000:5678:af23:00d5	2001::1234:0:5678:af23:d5

Table 2.8—IPv6 addresses compressed using both methods

IPv6 Addresses with an Embedded IPv4 Address

The third method of representation of an IPv6 address is to use an embedded IPv4 address within the IPv6 address. While valid, it is important to keep in mind that this method is deprecated and in fact considered obsolete because it is applicable only in the transition of IPv4 to IPv6.

Subnetting with IPv6

As you have already learned, IPv6 addresses are allocated to companies with a prefix. The host part of the address is always 64 bits, and the standard prefix is usually 48 bits or /48. This leaves 16 bits free for network administrators to use for subnetting.

Because the same rules apply to both IPv4 and IPv6, as far as network addressing is concerned, you can have only one network per network segment. You can't break the address and use some host bits on one part of the network and some on another.

If you look at the addressing in the chart below, the situation should make more sense:

Global Routing Prefix	Subnet ID	Interface ID
48 bits or /48	16 bits (65,536 possible subnets)	64 bits

Table 2.9—Bit allocation for IPv6 addresses

You need never concern yourself about running out of host bits per subnet because each subnet has over 18 quintillion hosts. It's unlikely that any organization would ever run out of subnets, but even if this were the case, another global routing prefix could easily be provided by the ISP.

Let's say, for example, that you are allocated the global routing prefix 0:123:abc/48. This address occupies three sections of a full IPv6 address, and each section or quartet is 16 bits, so you have 48 bits used so far. The host portion will require 64 bits, leaving you 16 bits for allocation as subnets.

You would simply start counting up in hex from zero (zero is legal) and keep going. For your hosts you would do the same, unless you wanted to reserve the first few addresses for servers on the segment, for example.

Let me use a simpler prefix for our example: 2001:123:abc/48. The first subnet would be all zeros, and of course, the first host on each subnet would be all zeros, which is legal (since you don't reserve the all 0s and all 1s addresses in IPv6). You would represent the all-zeros host by the abbreviated format using double colons.

Here are the first few subnets and host addresses:

Global Prefix	Subnet	First Address
2001:123:abc	0000	::
2001:123:abc	0001	::
2001:123:abc	0002	::
2001:123:abc	0003	::
2001:123:abc	0004	::
2001:123:abc	0005	::
2001:123:abc	0006	::
2001:123:abc	0007	::
2001:123:abc	0008	::
2001:123:abc	0009	::
2001:123:abc	000A	::
2001:123:abc	000B	::
2001:123:abc	000C	::
2001:123:abc	000D	::
2001:123:abc	000E	::
2001:123:abc	000F	::
2001:123:abc	0010	::
2001:123:abc	0011	::
2001:123:abc	0012	::
2001:123:abc	0013	::
2001:123:abc	0014	::
2001:123:abc	0015	::
2001:123:abc	0016	::
2001:123:abc	0017	::

Table 2.10—First few subnets and host addresses of 2001:123:abc/48

You have already noticed a difference from IPv4 addressing rules, I'm sure, in that you can use the all-zeros subnet and the first subnet address is always all zeros. Looking at a simple network topology, you could allocate the subnets in the below fashion:

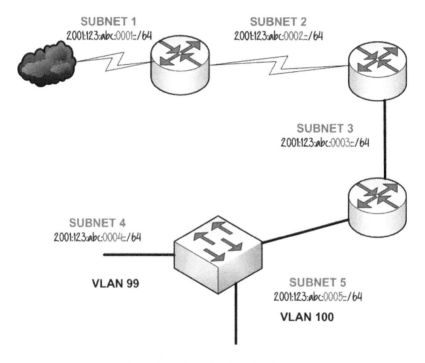

Fig. 2.5—Allocating IPv6 subnets

Can it really be that easy? If you recall from the IPv4 subnetting section, it can become somewhat of a nightmare to figure that out as well as to work out how many hosts and subnets there are and remember to exclude certain addresses. IPv6 subnetting is far easier. You may not be allocated a 48-bit prefix—it could be /56 for a home or smaller network—but the principle would be the same.

You can also subnet off the bit boundary, but it would be most unusual and unfair of Cisco to expect you to go into that amount of detail in the short amount of time you have in the exam. Hopefully, the exam won't be a mean attempt to catch you out, but you never know. Just in case, here is an example of a /56 prefix length address:

2001:123:abc:8bbc:1221:cc32:8bcc:4231/56

The prefix is 56 bits, which translates to 14 hex digits (14 × 4 = 56), so you know that the prefix will take you to the middle of a quartet. This is where you could make a mistake in the exam. You must zero-hex bits 3 and 4 in the quartet before the prefix breaks:

2001:123:abc:<u>8b00</u>:0000:0000:0000:0000/56

I've underlined the quartet where the bit boundary is broken. In haste and due to time pressure in the exam, you could well miss this important step. Remember that you would also abbreviate this address (the first host on the first subnet) to:

2001:123:abc:<u>8b00</u>::/56

If they do try to catch you out in the exam, it will probably be an attempt to have you remove the trailing zeros from the quartet before the bit boundary is broken:

2001:123:abc:<u>8b</u>::/56

The above abbreviation is illegal.

You can steal bits from the host portion to use for subnets, but there should never be a reason to and it would break the ability to use many of the features IPv6 was invented to utilize, including stateless autoconfiguration.

VARIABLE LENGTH SUBNETING MASKING (VLSM)

Although subnetting provides a useful mechanism to improve IP addressing issues, in the past, network administrators were able to use only one subnet mask for an entire network. RFC 1009 addressed this issue by allowing a subnetted network to use more than one subnet mask.

Think of it as being given a large slice of cake. You can cut that slice of cake into two (or more) pieces, or you could take one of the two slices and cut that into smaller slices. It's basically subnetting a subnet.

Today, a network administrator can have a Class B address with a 255.255.192.0 mask and further break down that subnet into smaller units with more masks, such as 255.255.224.0. Instead of writing out the subnets in decimal, engineers in the real world use something called a slash address, writing out how many bits are used for subnetting. Some examples of this are shown below:

255.255.0.0 can be expressed as /16 because there are 16 binary bits masked.

11111111.11111111.00000000.00000000 = 16 on or masked bits
255.255.192.0 can be expressed as /18 because there are 18 binary bits masked.
11111111.11111111.11000000.00000000 = 18 on or masked bits
255.255.240.0 can be expressed as /20 because there are 20 binary bits masked.
11111111.11111111.11110000.00000000 = 20 on or masked bits

It is best to illustrate this with an example, as in Figure 2.6 below:

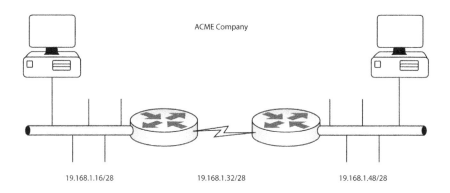

19.168.1.16/28   19.168.1.32/28   19.168.1.48/28

Fig. 2.6—ACME Company with no VLSM

You may have spotted a few problems with the addressing scheme above. The most important issue is the breach of the conservation of IP addresses.

If you are using RFC 1918 addresses (i.e., non-routable ones, such as 10.x.x.x), then perhaps you may not be worried about address wastage, but this is very bad practice, and for Cisco exams, you will be expected to conserve IP addresses.

With a /28 mask (or 255.255.255.240), you have 14 hosts per subnet. This may be fine for your LAN on either end, but for your WAN connection you need only two IP addresses, which wastes 12 addresses. You could change the masks to /30 (or 255.255.255.252), but then for your LANs you will obviously need more than two hosts.

The first workaround is to buy a separate network address for each network (two LANs and one WAN), but this would prove expensive and unnecessary. The other alternative is to break down the subnet further using VLSM, which is actually what it was designed to do!

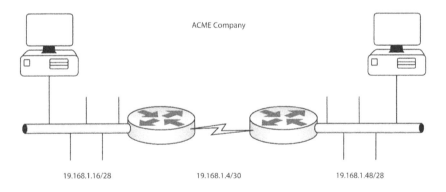

ACME Company

19.168.1.16/28   19.168.1.4/30   19.168.1.48/28

Fig. 2.7—ACME Company with VLSM

In Figure 2.7 above, you can see that the WAN link now has a /30 mask, which produces two usable hosts. You also have a tighter addressing allocation. If ACME Company expands (as companies often do), you can easily allocate further WAN links and LANs.

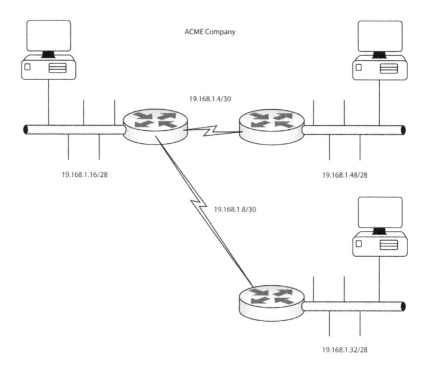

Fig. 2.8—ACME Company with a new office

In Figure 2.8 above, you can see that ACME Company has now grown and added a remote office. Because you have taken the time to plan and allocate a carefully thought out VLSM scheme, you can simply allocate the next block of IP addresses.

But will the IP addresses clash? This is a very common question, and it's a valid one. Let's say you have address 19.16.1.1/28 for one of your LANs. You will not therefore be able to use the IP address 19.16.1.1 with any other subnet mask. The IP address can be used only once, no matter which subnet mask is attached to it.

This is a bit of a head-scratcher for people who are new to networking or subnetting, but it does work. The general concept here is that VLSM does not remove the need for unique IP addresses; it just helps to efficiently manage their use.

VLSM PRACTICE

Here is a network you have been asked to design an addressing scheme for:

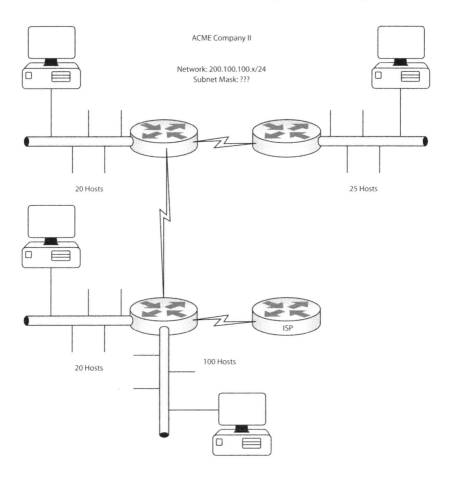

Fig. 2.9—ACME Company II

In Figure 2.9 above, ACME Company II has been allocated the 200.100.100.x network, with a default mask of 255.255.255.0. If you keep the standard mask, you will be left with one network with 254 usable hosts. Using the bottom half of the Subnetting Cheat Chart introduced earlier, tick down eight places in the Hosts - 2 column, which will give you one subnet with 256 - 2 hosts, or 254 hosts.

The challenge is this: You have three serial connections, and each requires only two usable host addresses. You also have four LANs that need between 20 and 100 hosts. If you design a mask to give you 20 to 100 hosts, you will be wasting a lot of addresses. To get 100 hosts, tick down seven places in the Hosts - 2 column, which will give you a mask of 255.255.255.128 (because you have only one bit left to tick down in the Subnets column). This gives you 126 hosts (128 - 2). You will then have two networks: one starting at 200.100.100.0 and one starting at 200.100.100.128. Not great, to be honest, because you need seven subnets (three WANs and four LANs) and some require only 20 hosts—so why waste 108 addresses?

Referencing the bottom half of the Subnetting Cheat Chart below, tick down in the Hosts - 2 column until you find a number close enough to give you 100 hosts. The only number you can use is 128, which is seven ticks down, so you are stealing 7 bits from the host portion, leaving you 1 bit for subnetting.

Powers of 2	Subnets	Hosts - 2
2	√	√
4		√
8		√
16		√
32		√
64		√
128		√
256		
512		

Using the upper part of the Subnetting Cheat Chart, tick down one place to reveal the subnet mask of 128.

Subnets	
128	√
192	
224	
248	
252	
254	
255	

When you use the 128 subnet with ACME Company II's IP address, you get subnet 200.100.100.0 and subnet 200.100.100.128, both with a mask of /25, or 255.255.255.128. For the network needing 100 hosts, you can use the 200.100.100.128 subnet. For the first host, you will use 200.100.100.129 and so on up to 200.100.100.229. So now you have:

200.100.100.128/25 – LAN (hosts 129-254)
200.100.100.0/25 – available for use or for VLSM

You need to allocate hosts to the three remaining LANs and the three WANs. The other three LANs all need between 20 and 30 hosts. If you tick down five places in the Hosts - 2 column, you will get 32 - 2, or 30 hosts. If you steal 5 bits from the host portion, you are left with 3 bits for the subnet (because there are 8 bits in every octet).

Powers of 2	Subnets	Hosts - 2
2	√	√
4	√	√
8	√	√
16		√
32		√
64		
128		
256		
512		

Tick down three places in the upper half of the Subnetting Cheat Chart to reveal the subnet mask of 224. This mask will give you eight subnets (you need only three for the LANs), and each subnet will have up to 30 available host addresses. Can you see how this will fit ACME Company II's requirements?

Subnets	
128	√
192	√
224	√
240	
248	
252	
254	
255	

If you tick across three places in the upper half of the Subnetting Cheat Chart, you will see that the subnets go up in increments of 32, so the subnets will be 0, 32, 64, and 96; you cannot use 128 because it was used for the large LAN.

Bits	128	64	32	16	8	4	2	1
	√	√	√					

So now you have:

200.100.100.0/27 – Reserve this for the WAN links.
200.100.100.32/27 – LAN 1 (hosts 33-62)
200.100.100.64/27 – LAN 2 (hosts 65-94)
200.100.100.96/27 – LAN 3 (hosts 97-126)

Next, you need IP addresses for the three WAN connections. WAN IP addressing is fairly easy because you need only two IP addresses if it is a point-to-point link. In the Hosts - 2 column, tick down two places to get 4 - 2, or two hosts. This leaves 6 bits for the subnet.

Powers of 2	Subnets	Hosts - 2
2	√	√
4	√	√
8	√	
16	√	
32	√	
64	√	
128		
256		
512		

Tick down six places in the upper half of the Subnetting Cheat Chart to get 252 as the subnet mask.

Subnets	
128	√
192	√
224	√
240	√
248	√
252	√
254	
255	

Network Addresses

As a network administrator, you will need to keep a record of the IP addresses and subnets that have been used. So far, you have allocated the following addresses:

WAN links

200.100.100.0/30 – WAN link 1 (hosts 1-2)
200.100.100.4/30 – WAN link 2 (hosts 5-6)
200.100.100.8/30 – WAN link 3 (hosts 9-10)

LAN hosts

200.100.100.32/27 – LAN 1 (hosts 33-62)
200.100.100.64/27 – LAN 2 (hosts 65-94)
200.100.100.96/27 – LAN 3 (hosts 97-126)

Large LAN hosts

200.100.100.128/25 – LAN (hosts 129-254)

CHOPPING DOWN

VLSM principles will let you take a network and slice it down into smaller chunks. Those chunks can then be sliced into smaller chunks and so on. You will reach the limit only when you get to the mask 255.255.255.252, or /30, because this gives you two usable hosts, which is the minimum you will need for any network.

Consider network 200.100.100.0/24. If you change the mask from /24 to /25, this is what happens:

Original mask (last octet)	00000000	1 subnet	254 hosts
New mask (Subnet 1)	00000000	200.100.100.0 – Subnet 1	126 hosts
New mask (Subnet 2)	10000000	200.100.100.128 – Subnet 2	126 hosts

Now you have two subnets. If you take the new Subnet 2 of 200.100.100.128 and break it down further by changing the mask from /25 to /26, you get this:

Original mask (last octet)	10000000	1 subnet	126 hosts
New mask (Subnet 1)	10000000	200.100.100.128 – Subnet 1	62 hosts
New mask (Subnet 2)	11000000	200.100.100.192 – Subnet 2	62 hosts

If you take the second subnet and break it down further by changing the mask from /26 to /28 (for example), you get this:

Original mask (last octet)	11000000	1 subnet	62 hosts
New mask (Subnet 1)	11000000	200.100.100.192 – Subnet 1	14 hosts
New mask (Subnet 2)	11010000	200.100.100.208 – Subnet 2	14 hosts
New mask (Subnet 3)	11100000	200.100.100.224 – Subnet 3	14 hosts
New mask (Subnet 4)	11110000	200.100.100.240 – Subnet 4	14 hosts

SUMMARY

Hopefully, this has helped you understand VLSM a bit more. It's no mystery, really. Please take the time to go over the examples above again, and then have a go at the challenge below.

ACME Company II has been allocated the address 200.10.200.x/24, as shown in Figure 2.10. You are required to design an addressing system so that hosts can be given IP addresses and the WAN links can be addressed with no wastage.

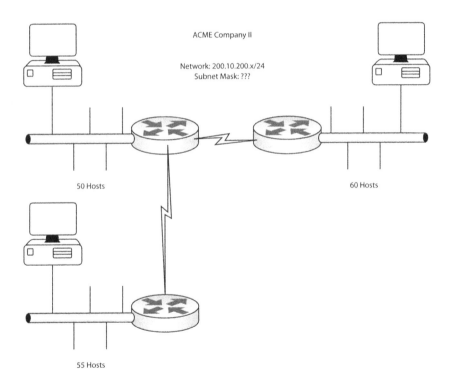

ACME Company II

Network: 200.10.200.x/24
Subnet Mask: ???

50 Hosts

60 Hosts

55 Hosts

Fig. 2.10—VLSM address allocation challenge

Congratulations!

Well done on getting this far! Subnetting is one of the necessary skills for network engineers, and yet it is also one of the most neglected. If you can confidently subnet, you're sure to be a useful addition to any network team or a valuable help to prospective clients as a network consultant.

Make sure you periodically review the book and videos (if you have access) to keep your subnetting skills sharp.

One last piece of advice: make sure you can write down the Subnetting Cheat Chart from memory for use in IT exams or interviews.

Paul Browning, November 2018
www.howtonetwork.com

Subnetting Resources

Books

101 Labs – IP Subnetting

Video Training

https://www.101labs.net – Training course for *101 Labs – IP Subnetting*

https://www.howtonetwork.com – Video training course matching this book (under TCP/IP)

RFCs

RFC 1918 – Address allocation for private internets

RFC 1219 – On the assignment of subnet numbers

RFC 950 – Internet standard subnetting procedure

RFC 940 – Toward an internet standard scheme for subnetting

RFC 932 – Subnetwork addressing scheme

RFC 917 – Internet subnets

The Subnetting Cheat Chart

	Bits	128	64	32	16	8	4	2	1
Subnets									
128									
192									
224									
240									
248									
252									
254									
255									
Powers of Two	Subnets	Hosts Minus 2							
2									
4									
8									
16									
32									
64									
128									
256									
512									
1024									
2048									
4096									
8192									
16384									